MW01232010

BEST BUDDIES
BIRTHDAYS

Also by Sarah (Sally) Butzin

Joyful classrooms in an age of accountability: The Project CHILD recipe for success. Phi Delta Kappa: Bloomington, IN, 2005

Project CHILD Teacher's Manual (revised). Institute for School Innovation: Tallahassee, FL, 2012

BEST BUDDIES BIRTHDAYS

The Complete Guide to Homegrown Parties for Ages 5-10

Sally Butzin and Charlotte Beal

ARCHWAY
PUBLISHING

Copyright © 2015 Sally Butzin and Charlotte Beal.

All rights reserved. No part of this book may be used or reproduced by any means, graphic, electronic, or mechanical, including photocopying, recording, taping or by any information storage retrieval system without the written permission of the publisher except in the case of brief quotations embodied in critical articles and reviews.

Archway Publishing books may be ordered through booksellers or by contacting:

Archway Publishing
1663 Liberty Drive
Bloomington, IN 47403
www.archwaypublishing.com
1 (888) 242-5904

Because of the dynamic nature of the Internet, any web addresses or links contained in this book may have changed since publication and may no longer be valid. The views expressed in this work are solely those of the author and do not necessarily reflect the views of the publisher, and the publisher hereby disclaims any responsibility for them.

Illustrations by Robert W. Smith.

ISBN: 978-1-4808-1822-4 (sc)
ISBN: 978-1-4808-1823-1 (e)

Library of Congress Control Number: 2015907733

Print information available on the last page.

Archway Publishing rev. date: 6/16/2015

Dedication

This book is dedicated with love to Sadie Beal, Tatum Beal, Madeline O'Reilly and Charlotte O'Reilly in the hope that their birthday parties will be a catalyst for Best Buddies Birthdays everywhere.

CONTENTS

PREFACE

We wrote this book as a mother/daughter team because we are both concerned about the trend toward excessive and over-commercialized birthday parties. What message does it send to children when parents feel compelled to compete for the most lavish party on the block? Large parties that include everyone in the class as well as adult guests can overshadow the birthday child and their special day

We know that many parents and grandparents feel as we do and are ready to scale back. But they also want their party to bring joy and satisfaction to their child. They need a detailed guide on how to plan and host a fabulous party. And kids need a hook to identify their party as unique from the Princess Party or Pirate Party. Now they can respond, "I'm having a Best Buddies Birthday party!"

Our book is the missing link. There are other party books on the market, but none as detailed and specific as Best Buddies Birthdays.

All the best buddies' activities have been field-tested with real kids, and have their stamp of approval. Today's tech-savvy kids still enjoy games that keep them active, involved, and successful. We want to bring back the joy and innocence of childhood, while instilling positive values. Our book gives parents permission to jump off the excessive celebration bandwagon.

ACKNOWLEDGEMENTS

Special thanks to Coach Justin Kurlander, Center Director Tracy Davis and all the kids at the Lafayette Park Recreation Center in Tallahassee, Florida, who helped field-test the games in this book. Justin and the kids gave insightful suggestions to improve activities to make them even more fun.

Also thanks to our illustrator Bob Smith, whose whimsical drawings capture the spirit of enjoying small parties with your best buddies.

And finally, hugs to Sadie and Tatum Beal who pioneered Best Buddies Birthdays in Burbank, California. Sadie invited her seven best buddies to celebrate her 8th birthday, while Tatum celebrated his 5th with four preschool friends. And their dad, Josh Beal, pitched in and made many valuable suggestions. The authors used these parties to make final tweaks to the book and put the icing on the cake, so to speak.

CHAPTER 1

INTRODUCTION

Are you concerned about:

- The over-commercialization of your kids' lives?
- Bullying and stressful school situations?
- Excessive competition (not just among kids, but among moms)?
- Your finances?
- Being a present and valuable role model for your kids?

If any of the above ring true, this book is for you!

America is undergoing a cultural, economic, and educational shift, and parents hold the power to be the trailblazers. Bling is out, and old-fashioned fun is in. Birthday parties, in a way, are a flashpoint—the symbol of much more than just a party.

Do children really need over-the-top birthday parties with pony rides, bounce houses, corporate movie characters, food trucks, and themed decorations? How about destination parties that require renting nail salons, skating rinks, restaurants, and video arcades? Over-the-top parties just lead to more stress, despite parents' understandable urge to outsource party planning.

You have the interest and willingness to tamp down the craziness, but until now you haven't had a guide to hold your hand. This book is our gift to you: a complete how-to guide to throwing a small, sane, yet totally scintillating birthday party for your five- to ten-year-old.

Do-it-yourself doesn't have to be complicated. The time is right for backyard or living room parties full of only close friends (aka best buddies) to flourish once again. Our book will enable you to simplify the planning while magnifying the enjoyment, all within a reasonable budget.

So who are we to hand you this roadmap? One of us is a lifelong elementary school educator, and one of us has two young children growing up in the one-upmanship wilds of Los Angeles, observing the party scene while tracking consumer behavior for her day job at a market research company.

When memes like #NailedIt start popping up all over, you know that people are desperate for a release valve. (Moms and would-be crafters are posting pictures of their failed baking and decorating creations on Pinterest with the sarcastic hashtag #NailedIt.) Writers like J.J. Keith, in her book *Motherhood Smotherhood*, are exposing "the cult of effort" that paralyzes moms. Some have expressed a need to escape the pressure coming from the "mom mafia" who compete to outdo each other's parties.

From the kids' perspectives, child development specialists like Betsy Brown Braun are cautioning against out-of-control birthday parties that spoil rather than celebrate. Books like *The Opposite of Spoiled*, by Ron Lieber, are helping parents instill smart money habits in their kids. And educational movements are promoting grit and perseverance rather than rewarding the end result or giving a trophy to everyone.

We see it all around us: You, the parents, are craving permission to jump off the excessive celebration escalator, just as we see you jumping off the consumption treadmill in other areas of life, such as buying "generics" over brand names, renting or recycling clothes, and making dinner more often than picking up takeout. You're also concerned about your children's overstressed school experience and supercharged after-school schedules, along with hours of homework, leaving little time for easygoing playing and relaxing. The time is right to simplify.

This book emphasizes the important life lessons that children learn through *Best Buddies Birthdays*, such as

- empathy,
- hospitality,
- graciousness,
- appreciation,
- good sportsmanship, and
- kindness.

Best Buddies Birthdays taps into young children's deep-seated need for security and familiarity. As every parent knows, their child will ask to hear the same bedtime story read over and over. What can be more comforting than being in your own home with a few close friends, playing games that children know by heart?

Oftentimes, parties are put on for the adults—complete with alcohol and alternative menus. They often seem designed more to impress other parents than to celebrate the child. This book encourages you to turn the tide by acknowledging that birthdays should be appropriately child-focused. In fact, we also recommend a return to drop-off parties to remove the pressure to entertain adult guests.

We also understand that in today's fragmented online world, birthday parties are sometimes the only chance that parents get to socialize with other parents. So you might consider an "after-party" where parents can hang out when they come to pick up their children. The parents can socialize (adult beverages and light snacks may be in order) while the children have free play.

Children will have just as much fun with old-fashioned games, simple activities, and cake with ice cream, where everyone feels welcome and successful. No need to provide elaborate meals with all the trimmings. The kids are too excited to eat much anyway.

Birthday parties should be a wonderful experience for the birthday child; it's about recognizing that they are special for who they are, not for what they have. When birthday parties become mob celebrations with frenetic commotion and guests the child hardly knows, or they drag on for too long without structure or focus on what the kids want, the birthday child can be reduced to tears as tempers are frayed.

As you've reached the end of this chapter, you may be saying, "Yes, I like the thought, but I could never pull that off." You may feel intimidated or even fearful of being in charge of a house full of young children, even with just a few best buddies. And that's why we have taken pains to give you a roadmap for tricks of the trade that master teachers use to keep young kids engaged and successful. Each chapter gives you step-by-step instructions from beginning to end. You can do it!

And for those of you who do enjoy putting on more elaborate parties, this book is also for you. Just skip right to chapter 5 for all the games and activities that will provide hours of fun for children ages five to ten; the information is great for playdates and neighborhood gatherings. All the activities in this book have been kid tested and kid approved.

We understand that *Best Buddies Birthdays* will require a little more effort than just outsourcing or hiring a professional entertainer. We acknowledge that it's tough to feel like the first person to blaze a trail. But our step-by-step directions and tips for success are sure to turn your next Best Buddies Birthday into an easy annual tradition for your family in no time. Soon the whole neighborhood will be on board.

Nostalgia, comfort, and sanity—here we come. Join the revolution!

CHAPTER 2

GETTING READY—PLANNING AND INVITATIONS

Whom Should I Invite?

Think small and blessedly simple! Consult with your child to include his or her special friends and close family members. The ideal Best Buddies Birthday should have no more guests than the child's age; for example, a five-year-old has five guests, or a ten-year-old has ten guests. Also, let your child decide whether to invite all boys, all girls, or a mixed group. The best mixture for successful parties is close friends regardless of gender. It is fine to have fewer guests than the child's age, just not more.

Do not succumb to pressure to invite the child's entire class and distant relatives. (Remember, you're a trailblazer here.) Large numbers just lead to more stress and less fun. You may worry that some children will be left out and feelings may be hurt. But this will surely become a moot point if you talk to your child about the importance of keeping their guest list confidential, which teaches your child humility in the process—a bonus!

Limiting the guests to your child's closest classmates and friends eliminates the chance that you will have to include the class bully or other children who your child may not like so much. Just because you are in the same class does not mean that you are best friends with everyone. Not even adults are best friends with everyone on their block or at their job. And besides, you will be setting a precedent that other parents will appreciate when they don't have to fork out money time after time for twenty to twenty-five birthday parties that include the entire class.

Now of course there will be exceptions, especially if your child is in a small class where everyone will be invited except one or two. We certainly don't want to promote cruelty and hurting others. Use your judgment.

While we're on the subject, don't invite your guests' parents or the child's adult relatives. Best Buddies Birthdays are for children only. You may ask a parent who you know well or a grandparent to help out if needed, but one additional adult is plenty. It may sound counterintuitive, but research shows that children behave better when fewer adults are present.

It's also important to specify that siblings of guests are not included. There may be parents who assume that the invitation applies to all of their children, or some who see this as an opportunity to have a few hours of free time while you watch all of their kids. But nothing can ruin a party more than a big brother or sister who dominates all the games at a six-year-old party.

And finally, what about the birthday child's siblings? Use your judgment, depending on the age differences and how they get along. It may be a good idea to send brothers and sisters to play elsewhere during the party so that the focus stays on the birthday child. Or give siblings specific helper jobs such as scorekeeper or judge. It is best if siblings do not participate in the games with the guests.

Where Should the Party Take Place?

In your home, of course—the perfect place for any time of year! Many of the activities provided in this book can be used either indoors or out in the backyard. But a word to the wise: Always have an indoor backup plan ready in case of rainy weather.

You may dread the cleanup, but calm your nerves by counting the number of dollars you'll be saving by NOT outsourcing the party, and by smugly dreaming of how well-adjusted your child may turn out as a grownup, having been saved from the world of insane, off-the-rails, over-the-top parties. And remember, our directions and tips ensure a simple, easy and accessible affair with not that many kids in attendance, which means that cleanup won't be that bad, anyway.

If you have pets, consider keeping them away from the party. Some of your guests may be allergic to cats or dogs or may be fearful. Best to put Fido in the yard and keep Fluffy in a closed room during the party.

Also consult with your professional insurance agent if you are concerned about liability issues in case of accidents. Most homeowners policies include a liability rider, but this may not be the case if you have renters insurance.

Time of Day?

Schedule the party for a Saturday or Sunday afternoon, even in the summertime, so as not to interfere with most parents' work schedules.

The ideal timeframe is between the hours of 1:30 PM and 4:30 PM (two hours max for the entire party). This will not interfere with mealtimes or church. Also children are often getting bored by the time the afternoon rolls around, and ready for some fun.

Party Theme?

Rest assured, there will be no hemming and hawing and brainstorming about which theme to choose and how to execute that theme. The theme for Best Buddies Birthdays is nothing but "Come and Have Fun!" Children will have just as much fun without elaborate decorations and over-priced movie character cups and napkins. For the kid who insists on yet another princess party, tell her you can watch the princess movie as a family on a special night, such as her actual birthday date.

Picture the party that your mom likely threw for you back when times were simpler. Hang some crepe paper and balloons, and maybe buy some festive paper plates and cups. Let the birthday child select decorations at the dollar store when you are shopping for game prizes. (More on that later.) This teaches math skills by working within a budget.

Party Agenda

The ideal Best Buddies Birthday lasts two hours. This is ample time for games, gifts, and refreshments. Here is a sample agenda. Details follow in Chapter 3.

Sample Agenda

2:00	Parents drop off guests
2:15	Welcome and assign jobs
2:30	Play game(s)
3:00	Eat birthday cake
3:15	Open gifts
3:45	Do a closing activity
4:00	Parents pick up guests
4:00-5:00	Optional after-party

Gifts

Specify on the invitation a limit on cost of birthday gifts—$20 max seems sane to us. Since you are only inviting close friends, they should know what the birthday child likes: books, stuffed animals, games, sporting equipment, etc. Or you can give some ideas of categories for gifts.

You can even suggest that guests pick out a gently used toy from their own stash, and wrap it for the birthday child. This teaches sharing and recycling.

Favors

We have yet more good news: You *do not* need to purchase take-home favors and/or party bags for a Best Buddies Birthday. The guests will be earning their "favors" as part of the games and activities. And besides, most of the trinkets that kids receive as favors usually wind up in the trash shortly after the party is over.

Consider instead taking a group photo that will be included as a remembrance when your child sends thank-you notes.

Prizes

The games and activities provided in this book offer opportunities for the guests to earn prizes. Determine your budget, and take your child to a dollar store to purchase small trinkets for prizes. Let the birthday child pick out items their friends would like. This enhances math skills by keeping within a budget. Purchase enough game prizes so that every guest will win at least one.

Refreshments

More relief in sight: In the coming new world order brought on by our book, there is absolutely no need to hire a caterer, order pizzas or cook up any savory food. Refreshments for a genuine Best Buddies Birthday mean nothing but cake and a drink – period. This also relieves much of the stress of determining any food allergies of any of the guests.

You can make a homemade birthday cake or cupcakes, or purchase as your budget permits. Let the birthday child determine the type and flavor they prefer. Ice cream is always a nice addition, but not essential. Also purchase birthday candles when you are at the dollar store.

For a drink, consider a punch or lemonade made with 100% fruit juice, or cut it with water at home. Nothing is more annoying than having to help each kid stick a straw into juice boxes or pouches, so buy larger containers (cheaper anyway) and pour out into cups at home. Rather than leaving out snacks and drinks for the kids to help themselves, serve cake and the drink at a designated time.

Sending Invitations

We like the idea of your child helping send out hard-copy invitations, because we want to preserve the dying act of snail mail, and because every kid loves getting a card in the actual mail. You can also deliver a backup to the parents via email, which encourages a quick reply.

Instead of purchasing blank invitations, you can create your own. See the sample below. You can also download invitation templates on your computer.

Don't pass out invitations at school, at after-school daycare, or any other public venue. Most schools have rules against this anyway, plus you will never know if the invitations actually make it home. This also eliminates the stigma of some students not getting invitations, since you are not inviting the entire class.

NOTE: If you plan on games that include water play or active running, be sure to indicate on the invitation that guests should wear bathing suits, bring a towel, or wear sneakers for running.

Sample Invitation

Dear _____

You are invited to my BEST BUDDIES BIRTHDAY PARTY.
Come celebrate on Saturday, March 7th, 1:30pm - 3:30pm
2000 Hill Street • Pleasant Town, 91000
Please come for fun, games and birthday cake.
I hope you can make it! Your friend,

Olivia Rodriquez
Please let me know yes or no by emailing parents@email.com.
Notes to Parents: Please drop off your child at 1:30 and pick up at 3:30.*
No siblings, please. Not all classmates are invited, so we're trying to encourage confidentiality.
Thank you!
*Optional: Parents, please stay for an after-party until 4:30.

Getting Responses

It is very important that you get an accurate head count for the party.
Your invitation should offer multiple ways to respond. If you do not get
a response within a few days of sending out the invitations, you should
follow up with a phone call or email until you get a firm yes or no.

Shopping List

You can purchase most of the items at a dollar store, grocery store,
or discount supermarket. You should be able to give a Best Buddies
Birthday for well under $100, especially if you make your own cake and
use washable plates, cups and silverware. Here are the basics:

- Note cards and envelopes (enough for invitations and thank-you notes)
- Stamps
- Name tags

- Simple decorations (crepe paper, balloons, etc.)
- Trinkets and/or candy for game prizes
- Game materials (as specified in the directions for the activity(s) you select)
- Special hat or crown for the birthday child
- Birthday cake or cupcakes
- Ice cream (optional)
- Birthday candles and matches or lighter
- Drinks
- Tablecloth (optional) or construction paper and markers for the guests to make their own placemats
- Plates
- Napkins
- Cups
- Forks and spoons
- Paper towels (in case of spills)
- 3x5 cards to make job cards
- Paper bag to hold the job cards
- Camera
- Kitchen timer (to stay on schedule with activities)
- Paper/pencil to write parent emergency contact numbers

CHAPTER 3

GIVING THE PARTY

Assuring Success

The goal for a Best Buddies Birthday is that all the guests leave with smiles on their faces. Even better is for them to say, "Wow, that was the best party I've ever been to!"

So how can you assure success? This chapter will give you some tips on pacing and keeping young children engaged and involved. Busy children are happy children. Successful children are happy children. So you need to keep everyone busy and assure they all have successful experiences.

Set Up

Before the guests arrive, you need to "party-proof" your house. Close doors to any rooms that are off-limits. Put any breakable items away and out of reach. Lay sheets or towels under craft tables and food tables if you are concerned about spills and such.

It is also a good idea to keep pets away from the party. Some children are afraid of dogs or allergic to cats—just another distraction and potential disruption to avoid.

Pre-Party Check List

Do a final check of the supplies needed when the guests arrive. Be sure to also have all the materials handy for the games and activities you have chosen, as well as refreshments.

Pre-Party Check List

- Name tags and magic markers
- Small slips of paper or notecards with jobs for the guests
- Paper bag or small box for the job cards
- Construction paper for making placemats (optional)
- Prize collection bags
- Special hat or crown for the birthday child (optional)
- Birthday candles and lighter
- Plates, silverware, napkins, cups
- Kitchen timer (to stay on schedule)
- Camera
- Paper/pencil to write parent emergency contact numbers

Print out the schedule for the party for yourself to use as a guide/reminder. Set the cake table and set up the games/activities. Write names on the prize bags.

Pre-Party Rehearsal and Adult Roles

It's a good idea to practice the games and activities you have chosen prior to the party. Also be sure to designate adult roles, such as who is running the game and giving directions. It gets confusing if one parent is explaining the game, and the other parent or grandparent interjects additional comments.

Sample Best Buddies Birthday Schedule

2:00	Parents drop off guests; welcome activity
2:15	Set expectations and assign jobs
2:30	Play games
3:00	Serve birthday cake
3:15	Open gifts
3:45	Do a closing activity (optional to fill time)
4:00	Parents pick up guests
4:00-5:00	Optional after-party for parents

Welcome Activity

As the guests arrive, you and the birthday child will open the door and welcome them warmly. Tell them where to put their wrapped gifts, and direct them to a specific spot where a welcome activity is ready. An adult will be monitoring this space and getting the activity started until all the guests arrive. **Be sure to write down an emergency contact number for each of the parents before they leave.**

The welcome activity keeps the guests busy until everyone arrives. However, if after about 5-10 minutes you're still waiting for just one last guest, go ahead and proceed to the first game.

A good welcome activity is to make name tags. This will also help you interact with each guest if you don't know them as well as your child does. Have the birthday child make a special name tag prior to the guests' arrival since he will be greeting arrivals at the front door.

Set up a table with sticky-back name tags that you can purchase at a dollar store or business supply store. Provide colored markers or crayons. Depending on the guests' ages, they can write their own names and decorate, or you can have names already printed for the guests to decorate.

You can also provide large sheets of construction paper for the guests to make their own placemats for birthday cake time. They can write their names and decorate as with the name tags.

Have some quiet music playing in the background to set the tone for a happy time ahead. You can choose popular children's music, or even introduce them to some classical music, which can soothe the soul (and calm your nerves in preparation for the two hours ahead!).

Set Expectations and Ground Rules for Behavior

As soon as all the guests have arrived and everyone has finished the welcome activity, you are ready to set expectations and lay down the ground rules for behavior. Since most guests will have never been to a Best Buddies Birthday, explain first what they will be doing. "Boys and girls, welcome to our home and to Arthur's Best Buddies Birthday. First we will be playing some games, then having refreshments, and finally opening presents. Then it will be time for your parents to pick you up."

Next explain your expectations for behavior. Do this in a positive manner. Tell the children what you want them to do, not what you don't want them to do. Children will tune out with a laundry list of don'ts.

Adults sometimes expect children to know how to behave. Don't assume that they have the same rules at home as you may have for your own children. You need to explain your rules to avoid any mishaps. Keep it simple and keep it positive.

Gather the kids together in a circle on the floor or grass. Introduce yourself and any adult helpers, and tell the children what you would like them to call you (Ms. Sally, Charlotte, etc.) You can wear a name tag as well. Have the children introduce themselves to you and to others who may not know them (in case of a cousin or sibling, for example). Remember that your objective is to make everyone feel comfortable, included and welcome. And of course you're also teaching some manners as well.

Begin the discussion by stating something like, "Hello, boys and girls. We are so glad you could come to Arthur's birthday party. Before we start the games, I want to tell you some rules so that everyone stays safe and has a good time. After I've finished, I may ask you to repeat some of them, so be sure to listen carefully."

Here are some suggestions for ground rules:

1. Explain the boundaries of where the guests are expected to go, and which areas are off limits, such as any rooms with a closed door.
2. Tell them to ask for permission to go to an off-limits area, or the bathroom.
3. Stay with the group.
4. Walk, don't run.
5. Speak with a soft voice that carries no farther than six inches. (In other words, no shouting or yelling.)
6. Keep your hands to yourself. (In other words, no pushing or shoving.)
7. Take turns and follow the rules for the games.

It is always a good idea to ask the children to repeat back to you what you just told them. This helps you clarify any misunderstandings. And be sure to project an inviting persona so that children feel free to ask for help if they need it.

Give Everyone a Job

Children feel successful when they feel useful. We suggest that you assign everyone a job as part of the ground rules talk. Have jobs written on extra name tags or small notecards and put in a paper bag. Have the guests take turns drawing a job from the bag and write their name on it or stick it on their shirt. This will help you remember whom to ask when a job needs to be done.

Here are some sample jobs. Choose jobs appropriate for the age group. All jobs will require some supervision.

- Hand sanitizer squirter
- Napkin folder
- Forks and spoons distributor
- Cake server
- Ice cream scooper
- Drink server
- Table clearer
- Gift wrap collector
- Gift list writer (listing who gave what for later thank-you notes)

Play the Games

Now it's time to start the games and activities. Be sure to have everything ready in advance. The activities provided in Chapter 5 of this book list all the materials you will need, as well as directions and rules. We also suggest that you practice before giving the party.

Depending upon age, you might consider having the birthday child describe the game and go over the rules. Most children love to be the leader, and what better time than on their birthday?

Have small bags for each child with their name written on it. They will use these to collect their prizes earned during the games. At the end of game time, have them put their bags near the entry door so they will remember to take them home at the end of the party.

Also be sure to have a timer so that you know when to end the games. You want to have plenty of time for birthday cake and opening presents. Review the agenda in Chapter 2 for suggested time frames.

Sing Happy Birthday and Eat Cake!

Now the children move to the table or other area you have designated for refreshments. The birthday child sits at the head of the table or in a special place. A special hat or "crown" is always a nice touch for the birthday child.

Ask the children who have jobs assigned to help you pass out silverware, plates and cups, fold napkins, and serve drinks. Remember to give every child a squirt of hand sanitizer prior to eating.

Everyone sings "Happy Birthday" and the birthday child blows out the candles. And we probably don't need to remind you to take lots of pictures. A group shot will also make a nice remembrance to send with the thank-you notes.

An adult should cut the cake into slices and put them on plates for the helper to serve to the guests. If you've assigned an ice cream scooper, they can add a scoop to each plate.

As with the welcome activity, have some soft joyful music playing in the background. Let the children enjoy some conversation while they eat.

Open the Gifts

Best Buddies Birthdays acknowledge the importance of giving and gratitude. We dislike the current trend of opening gifts after all the guests have gone home. This takes away the joy of giving and receiving. So we want you to make a ceremony out of opening the gifts. But only open gifts from the guests. Save family gifts or other gifts for another time during the day.

If you have assigned jobs for collecting the wrapping paper and listing the gifts and givers for future thank-you notes, remind the guest assigned of their job. Otherwise, you will need to note the gift list yourself.

Have the children sit in a circle with the wrapped gifts in the center. The birthday child will choose a gift, open it, acknowledge it gratefully, and proceed to the next gift. You might need to have a little practice session prior to the party, especially for young children. Role play how they will be gracious and grateful, even if it is a gift they may already have or don't especially like.

It is also fun to pass the gifts around the circle after each is unwrapped so all the guests get a close-up view. We don't recommend opening boxes and playing with gifts at this time. Save that for after the guests have left.

You can also take a picture of each guest standing next to the birthday child with their gift. These can be printed and included in the thank-you notes later.

Do a Closing Activity as You Wait for Pickups

By this time it should be almost time for parents to pick up their children. If you have some time left, or if some parents are late, have a final activity ready. This can be as simple as putting on a DVD of a children's show or movie. There are also some great kid karaoke DVD's that are fun. See also some suggested "time fillers" in Chapter 5.

Be sure to take a group photo if you didn't capture the moment during cake time.

The main thing is: Don't let your guard down until all the guests have gone. Keeping kids busy prevents trouble and possible rough-housing that will cause your wonderful party to end on a sour note.

Optional After-Party

Many parents will enjoy some time to socialize with other parents before leaving. Consider extending the party by offering drinks and light snacks for parents to enjoy while the children continue with free play for another hour. You will be tired by this time, so be sure to specify the timeframe for leaving so that no one overstays their welcome.

Say Goodbye

The birthday child should stay by the door and personally say goodbye to each guest and thank them for coming. Be sure that guests take their prize bag and any additional trinkets or candy that you want to include.

Relax and Smile

Now it's time to give your birthday child a big hug and sink into a comfortable chair (maybe with an adult beverage in hand?).You did it! You gave your child the best gift of all – a Best Buddies Birthday with memories to last until next year.

CHAPTER 4

FOLLOW UP

A few days have now passed, and it's time to put the icing on the cake.

One of the best lessons you can teach your child is gratitude. Sending thank-you notes is so important to model good manners and appreciation. You should send thank-you's no later than one week after the party.

As with invitations, we suggest that old-fashioned mailed thank-you notes provide a very classy finale to your Best Buddies Birthday. E-mail messages can also work, but there's nothing like getting something to open in the mail.

Have the birthday child review the list that you compiled of the gifts each guest brought. Depending on age and writing ability, the birthday child can write the notes entirely, or dictate for you to write. At the very least, they should be able to sign their name to make it personal.

You can purchase pre-printed thank-you notes at a dollar store. Any kind of note card will do. Here is a sample message.

Sample Thank-You Note

Dear_____,

Thank you for coming to my Best Buddies Birthday and for giving me _____. I really like it.
Your friend, _____

Pictures

It makes a nice memento to include a picture from the party in the thank-you card. If you have a group picture, send that. Or you may have taken a picture with each individual guest along with their gift with the birthday child.

Write the date of the party on the back. This will jog memories in later years when someone asks, "When was that really fun Best Buddies Birthday that I went to years ago?"

CHAPTER 5

GAMES AND ACTIVITIES

The games and activities in this chapter suggest the approximate time to complete each one. You will need to fill about 30 minutes of total game time. We also suggest picking one "time filler" or closing activity for the last 15 minutes of the party in case there is some time to spare. Better safe than sorry.

Attention Spans

Choose games or activities that fit the attention spans of the age group attending the party. Some child development experts suggest it is the child's age plus ten. In other words, a party for six-year olds should break into chunks of about 15 minutes (two 15-minute games), while ten-year olds can go for at least 30 minutes. Younger children can probably go longer than 15 minutes for more active games.

The games and activities are organized by age groups, as well as indoor or outdoor, active or creative and with suggested time frames. Use your judgment as you select activities by using attention span as your guide.

What Will Interest the Guests?

Be sure to consult with the birthday child to select games and activities that sound like fun to him or her. Discuss their friends' interests to determine which will hold their attention. Some children enjoy arts and crafts, while others prefer sports.

Avoid gender stereotyping. There are boys who like arts and crafts and girls who like sports. Let your child be the judge. That is why the activities in this book avoid being labeled for girls or boys.

Keeping Competitions Fair

A big part of assuring success is giving everyone a fair chance to compete and win in the games selected. The activities in this chapter give all guests a chance to win a prize and be successful.

Nothing spells disaster more than some guests feeling like left-out losers. For example, while piñatas are often used at birthday parties, we have not included them. Too often a few aggressive kids dominate the activity and rush in to scoop up the scattered prizes, leaving the mild-mannered kids on the sidelines.

Keeping Everyone Involved

Another tip to keep children engaged and focused is to avoid activities that eliminate children from the game. For example, "musical chairs" is a time-honored game at birthday parties. However, the game proceeds with children being eliminated as a chair is removed when the music stops. So now you have children standing around and out of the fun.

We have provided activities that will keep everyone in the game until the end. We have even adapted a type of musical chairs game with the twist of keeping everyone in the game until the end.

Neat Freaks, Beware

Let's face it, not everyone enjoys cooking or art projects that may require a lot of clean-up. Young kids do make messes. They spill and break things accidentally.

We want you to enjoy your Best Buddies Birthday as much as your guests. So choose activities that conform to your level of tolerance for messiness.

Activities Index

Denotes time filler. (These activities require little preparation and are good to have as extra choices in case you need to fill some time waiting for parent pick-ups.)

ACTING OUT

Category: Creative
Venue: Indoor or Outdoor
Time: 15-30 minutes
Ages: 5-10
Materials:

- Prizes (1 per guest) – perhaps something similar to the Oscar statue for movies
- Props (a variety of hats, wigs, scarves, neckties, shirts, skirts, etc.) Note that props are optional, but actors always enjoy dressing up a little.
- Note cards with suggested scenes or topics

Preparation:
The venue will be a circle of chairs for each guest, or sitting in a circle on the floor. The performers will be in the middle of the circle, so there needs to be room to move around a little.

Prepare some sample topic cards; at least one for each guest. Some suggestions are listed below.

Begin the Activity:
Tell the guests they are going to take turns acting out various scenes and topics for the audience to guess. Let their imaginations run wild. They can use props, or not; whatever they choose. The audience should not shout out their answers even if they think they know. (You may have to remind them several times as children get caught up in their enthusiasm and blurt out the answer.) They must stay silent until you ask them to guess. This will keep the activity going on longer.

The birthday child will go first. Proceed around the circle until everyone has had at least one turn. If there are guests who do not want to participate, they can pass. Usually the reluctant child will eventually join in as they see others do it, but do not force it.

The actor spends a minute or two performing in the middle of the circle. At the end, ask the seated children in the audience if they can guess what the actor depicted?

The children can make up their own scenes to act out, or select from cards you have prepared. Choose topics appropriate for the age level of the guests. Before beginning their skit, they tell the general category; for example, "This is a movie," or "This is a type of animal." However unlike charades, the actor may speak or sing.

Here are some sample skit topics:
Movie: Frozen; Little Mermaid; Lion King
Book: Little Red Riding Hood; Charlotte's Web; Goldilocks and the Three Bears
Animal: Elephant; Snake; Lion
Character: A scary monster; a pirate; cowboy
Action: Driving a car; riding a horse; swimming

Continue acting and guessing until everyone has had at least one turn. Then you can award prizes. Each guest who successfully performed a skit gets a *best actor* prize. Then if there were any reluctant guests who chose not to perform, they get a *good guesser* award.

ANIMAL CAPERS

Category: Quiet Games
Venue: Indoor
Time: 15 minutes
Ages: 5-7
Materials:

- Stuffed animals (In the invitation, ask that each guest bring their favorite stuffed animal. Have a few extra on hand in case someone forgets.)
- CD player and CD of marching music
- Light-weight blanket or sheet
- Paper and pencil for taking notes
- Prizes (1 per guest)

Preparation:
Move furniture to the edge of a large room to make space for the animal parade. You may allow the parade to go to several rooms; your choice. Have the other materials on hand.

Begin the Activity:
There are three parts to this activity. First the children will sit in a circle on the floor. Starting with the birthday child they will talk about their animal, telling its name and other information they want to share. Tell the children to listen carefully because they will need to remember the names later in the game. You will need to take notes so you remember as well. Then they take turns passing their animal around the circle for each child to hold and see. At the end, conduct a brief review to say each animal's name.

The children will then march around the room for an animal parade, marching to the music you will play. The birthday child is the leader, with the others following where he or she goes. If you wish to use several rooms for the parade, that is up to you. When the music stops, the children freeze, and will change the position of their animal on your command. They continue the parade when the music starts.

Repeat as needed. Here are some suggestions for variations. Let the children offer some carry positions as well. They will come up with silly ones for sure.

- March with your animal on your shoulder.
- March with your animal on your head.
- March holding your animal in one hand.
- March holding your animal around your neck.
- March with your animal behind your back.

For the third and final part of the game, the children return to the circle and sit on the floor with their animal. You will collect all the animals and place them in the center of the circle. Cover the pile of animals with a blanket or sheet.

One by one, starting with the birthday child, each guest goes to the blanket and reaches under to retrieve an animal. They hold it up and ask, "Whose animal is this?" The owner raises her hand and then chooses a child in the circle to tell the animal's name. The other children can give hints. When someone correctly remembers the name, they get a prize.

Continue retrieving an animal from under the blanket and having the owner choose a guest to guess its name. Remind the children to choose a guesser who has not yet won a prize. The game is over when all the animals are back with their rightful owner and everyone has a prize.

ARCADE GAMES

Category: Action

Venue: Indoor or Outdoor

Time: 30 minutes

Ages: 5-10

Materials:

- Prizes (at least 1 per guest)
- Game tickets (small slips of colored paper or purchased raffle-type tickets); 5 per guest
- 2 empty plastic bottles with a 1-inch opening, such as juice bottles
- 25 pennies
- 10 wooden clothes pins
- 6 empty glass soda bottles
- 5 embroidery rings or similar size plastic rings
- 1 fishing pole (yard stick or similar size stick with a string attached and a magnet on the end)
- 10 paper fish (made from construction paper) with a paperclip attached
- 1 large cardboard box or empty plastic child's swimming pool
- 1 deck of playing cards
- 1 standard 3 ½ gallon bucket
- 1 kitchen timer for the fishing game

Preparation:

Set up the arcade stations either in a large room inside or a large space outside. The children will move as a group from station to station to play the games.

Coin Drop

This station will have an empty plastic bottle and 25 pennies available. The object of the game is to stand over the bottle and drop a designated number of pennies into the bottle from at least waist high. For example, a 5-year-old needs to successfully drop 5 pennies, while a 10-year-old must get at least 20. You decide what is fair, yet challenging.

Clothes Pin Drop

This station will have an empty plastic bottle and clothes pins available. The object is to stand over the bottle and drop a designated number of clothes pins into the bottle, similar to the coin drop game. Younger children can hold the clothes pin closer to the bottle, while the older kids may have to drop it from nose high. You decide what is fair, yet challenging.

Bottle Ring Toss

This station will be set up with 6 glass soda bottles in an array of 1 in front, 2 behind that, 3 behind that, about 8 inches apart from each other. Rings for tossing will be available. Each child will stand at least 3 feet away (farther for older children) and successfully ring a designated number of bottles. You decide what is fair, yet challenging.

Fishing Challenge

This station will be set up with the paper fish laid out inside a cardboard box or plastic pool. The fish should be placed about 5 inches from each other. A fishing pole will be available for catching the fish. Each child will attempt to catch a fish by touching the magnet to the paperclip. The object is to catch a designated number of fish within a one or two minute time period. As before, vary the difficulty according to the age of the guests.

Card Toss

This station will be set up with a bucket and a deck of cards for tossing. The player stands at least three feet away from the bucket and flips the cards one at a time into the bucket. Vary the difficulty depending on the age group. Older children must stand farther back and get more cards in the bucket than the younger children.

Begin the Activity:

Move as a group to the first arcade station. The children will take turns at each station playing the game. You will serve as the judge. The birthday child can decide who will go first at each station and the order of play thereafter.

At each station you will tell the objective and rules for the game. You will award a ticket to each child who successfully completes the task. If a child does not get a ticket, they can come back again after they have visited all the stations and try again.

After all the stations have been completed, let the children select a prize based on the number of tickets they have earned. Be sure that everyone has at least one ticket for a prize. Second and third tries are OK.

BALLOON CHALLENGES

Category: Active

Venue: Outdoor

Time: 30 minutes

Ages: 8-10

Materials:

- Round balloons (5-10 per guest)
- Large garbage bags to hold the balloons
- Rope or tape for a starting line and finish line
- Roll of twine, cut into one-foot pieces (1 per guest)
- Score sheet and pencil
- Prizes (1 per guest)

Preparation:

Determine the playing field, which should be a large grassy area. Mark one end of the field with a line for the starting line, and another line opposite on the far side for the finish line. Blow up and tie the balloons and secure them in large garbage bags. (You can wait to blow them up when the activity begins and let the children help if you think they are capable.)

Begin the Activity:

There are three parts to these challenges. The children will work in teams to complete them. Divide the guests into two teams by counting off. The birthday child will be the captain of one team, and the guest with the closest birthday will captain the other team. The captains go to the starting line and stand about five feet from each other. The others line up behind their team captain in alphabetical order. If there is an uneven number, the captain of the team with one fewer player gets an extra turn.

The first challenge is to hop to the finish line with a balloon between your legs. If the balloon breaks you must go back to start and get another balloon. If it comes loose without breaking, you can retrieve it and keep going. When the hopper gets to the finish line, the next in line starts hopping to the finish line, and so on. The team that gets all players to the finish line first scores a point for each member of the team.

After the first challenge, you may scramble up the teams, or let the same teams compete. We suggest you scramble them if it is obvious that one team is superior.

For the second challenge, the object is to kick a balloon to the finish line. No hands allowed. Again, if a balloon breaks, go back to start and get a new balloon. Take turns as before until one team gets everyone across the finish line. Score a point for each member of that team.

For the final challenge, the object is to stomp on and break the balloon tied to an opposing team member's ankle. The children should be barefoot for this challenge to avoid any injuries.

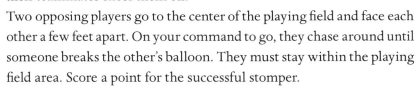

Tie a balloon to each child's ankle using the twine. The children go in pairs, while their teammates cheer them on.

Two opposing players go to the center of the playing field and face each other a few feet apart. On your command to go, they chase around until someone breaks the other's balloon. They must stay within the playing field area. Score a point for the successful stomper.

Award prizes based on points earned, with the most points choosing first from the prize pot.

BASKETBALL BASEBALL

Category: Active

Venue: Outdoor (or an indoor gym)

Time: 15-30 minutes

Ages: 8-10

Materials:

- Basketball hoop
- Basketball or soccer ball
- Spray paint (washable) to mark boundaries and bases (or small pieces of wood)
- Poster board and marker for scoreboard
- Prizes (1 per guest)

Preparation:

You will need a large secured driveway (not near a street) with a basketball hoop, or set up a portable hoop in a large grassy area.

Mark off three bases like a baseball diamond. Mark the foul lines. Home plate will be marked under the basketball hoop.

Begin the Activity:

Divide the guests into two teams by counting off. The team with the birthday child will "bat" first. The others are the fielding team. If a team has fewer players than the other, they will get an extra out.

The fielding team can position themselves anywhere on the playing field, or cover the bases. The game begins with the first "batter" going to home plate (under the basket) and throwing the ball into the playing field and running to first base. A player on the fielding team catches the ball and runs toward the basket, attempting to make a basket before the running player reaches a base. When the basket is made, the running player must stop on the closest base, or get all the way back to home plate for a home run if the fielder cannot make the basket. The players can use strategy, such as passing the ball to a teammate to attempt the basket, or throwing the ball softly to fool the fielding team who may be expecting a long throw.

Players earn a point for their team by getting all around the bases and back to home plate. When the fielding team has made three baskets, the batting team is out and they change places with the fielding team. Any player who deliberately throws out of bounds will be charged an out for their team.

Continue for five innings, or until time is up. The winning team will get first choice at the prize pot, and the losing team chooses last.

BEAN BAG TOSS

Category: Active

Venue: Indoor or Outdoor

Time: 30 minutes

Ages: 8-10

Materials:

- Fabric cut into 5x10 inch pieces (one per guest)
- Large sewing needles and thread (one per guest)
- Scissors to cut the thread
- Bags of small dried beans from the grocery store (enough to fill as many bags as you are making)
- Large bowl to hold the beans
- Three cardboard boxes (about the size of a cereal box)
- Magic marker
- Score sheet and pencil
- Tape or string for the starting line
- Prizes (1 per guest)

Preparation:

Cut off one large side of each box to create targets to capture the bean bags. Use the magic marker to write a large numeral inside each box, as well as around the sides of each box. One box will have a large 10, the second will have a large 50, and the third will have 100. These will be the targets to use for the bean bag toss contest.

You will set the boxes in a large open area with the open side facing up about five feet from each other, with the 10 box the closest to the starting line and the 100 the farthest.

Put the other materials in the center of a table where the children will work to make their bean bags. Pour the beans into a large bowl. Thread the needles in advance, one per guest.

Begin the Activity:

Tell the children they will each need to make a bean bag to use in the upcoming bean bag contest. Show them how to fold the fabric together with the short ends together and sew together along two sides. (You might want to have a sample done with two sides already sewn.) Then they will fill their bag with beans, and sew the last side together to secure the beans. (You may need to help knot the thread at the end.) When everyone has finished, proceed to the contest area.

The birthday child goes first, and the others line up according to their birthday months. Each contestant gets a turn to toss all the beanbags toward the boxes. Any beanbag that goes into a box scores that many points. Bags that hang on the side do not count.

Set a challenge goal of 300 points or so to earn a prize. Continue taking turns until everyone has accumulated at least the minimum number of points. After the first round, adjust the distance of the target boxes if you find they are too easy or too difficult.

Then the guests choose a prize from the prize pot with the child who scored the highest getting first choice, and so on.

BURIED TREASURE

Category: Active
Venue: Outdoor (best) or Indoor
Time: 30 minutes
Ages: 8-10
Materials:

- Prizes that will serve as the treasure (1 per guest)
- Small bags or box to hold the treasure (1 per team)
- Writing paper for making the maps
- Markers and pencils
- Kitchen timer

Preparation:
Gather the treasure bags or boxes and map-making materials. Have them ready to begin the activity. Determine the boundaries if outside, or what rooms are to be used if inside.

Begin the activity:
Have the children count off to form teams of two or three persons. Give each team their bag or box with the treasures inside and the map-making materials.

Send the teams off to their designated boundaries. If outside: one team to the front yard; another to the back; another to the side. If inside: each team goes to a separate room. The key is to have each team out of sight of the others.

Set the timer for 15 minutes. The teams must hide their treasure and then make a map for the other teams to discover it. The maps can use visual directions or written clues. For example,

"Start at the swing set and walk ten paces to your left."
"Face the back porch and walk toward the tallest pine tree."

Etc.

When the timer goes off after 15 minutes, the teams must all return to home base. One team at a time will give one other team their map and go with them to oversee the treasure hunt. Everyone can go to watch if there are more than two teams.

The hunting team must follow the map and/or clues to find the hidden treasure. If they find it, they get to keep it. The team that made the map can give clues and hints if the hunting team is having trouble reading the map. But ideally, there should be no talking unless the hunting team is truly floundering.

CHALLENGES IN A BOTTLE

Category: Active

Venue: Indoor or Outdoor

Time: 15-30 minutes depending on the number of challenges

Ages: 5-7

Materials:

- Plastic soda or juice bottle with large opening
- Note cards or small slips of paper
- Pen or marker
- Prizes (1 per guest)

Preparation:

On small note cards or slips of paper, write the challenges. Samples are given below, plus you can add your own. The older the children, the more challenging the tasks can be. Make them difficult, but not impossible. Let your birthday child make up some to challenge the guests.

Fold the written challenges and put them inside the bottle. Fold them small enough so they can be shaken out of the bottle. (Be sure the inside of the bottle is dry so that the cards don't stick.) Screw on the top.

Sample challenges:

1. Rub your tummy and pat your head at the same time for 30 seconds
2. Hug two children
3. Hop on one foot while counting to five (or more for older children)
4. Shake hands with three children
5. Act like a cat or dog
6. Act like a snake
7. Walk in a circle behind the guests while patting your head
8. Walk backwards around the circle while patting your head

9. Sing the happy birthday song
10. Shout "happy birthday" 10 times in your loudest voice
11. Count to ten (or more) in a whisper
12. Act like a very scary monster

Begin the Activity:

Have the children sit in a large circle on the floor with plenty of space in the middle to perform the challenge. Place the bottle in the middle of the circle.

Note: If there are shy children who are reluctant to participate, assure them they can be *watchers* until they are ready to play. Let each child state whether they want to be a *watcher* or *player*. Most of the watchers quickly change their minds after they see how much fun it is.

The birthday child starts the activity by spinning the bottle until it stops. Whoever it points to will pick up the bottle, open it, and shake out a challenge card. The child will read it (or you can read it if the child is a non-reader) and then perform the task. The child also has the option to pass. The children in the circle will respond with thumbs up if the task was performed correctly, or thumbs down if not. If thumbs-up wins, the child keeps the card.

The child who just completed the task will close the bottle and spin it again for the next task challenge. Proceed as above until all the challenges have been performed. If the spinning bottle stops at a child who has already had a turn, spin again. Be sure that everyone gets at least one turn.

After all the challenge cards are gone, the guests tally up their cards. Everyone who has at least one card (which should be everyone) gets a prize.

CHASING GAMES

Category: Active

Venue: Outdoor or Indoor

Time: 15 minutes (time filler)

Ages: 5-7

Materials:

- Cloth napkin or handkerchief
- Prizes (1 per guest)

Preparation:

These classic children's games require no preparation, and so can be good time fillers for the younger children if you have extra time to spare.

Begin the Activity:

The children sit in a large circle on the floor or grass. Be sure there is room behind the circle for the children to run. There are three parts to these chase games.

The first is the classic Duck, Duck, Goose. The birthday child goes first, and walks around the circle behind the sitting children while gently tapping each on the head and saying, "duck, duck, duck, etc." But when he says "goose," the child who was tapped has to get up and chase the tapper around the circle and back to his spot. If the chaser tags the tapper, the chaser goes back to his spot and earns a point. The tapper goes again. If the tapper safely gets back to the spot without being tagged, he earns a point. The chaser becomes the next tapper. Continue until everyone has had at least one turn to be the tapper.

The second chase is Drop the Hanky. On this chase the birthday child again goes first, walking around the back of the circle holding the hanky (napkin or handkerchief). Then he drops it behind one of the seated children, who gets up, picks up the hanky, and chases the child who dropped the hanky. The object is to get back to the spot without getting tagged. Proceed as before with awarding points until everyone has a turn to drop the hanky.

The third chase is Pop Goes the Weasel. The tune is well known for toy jack-in-the-boxes. For this game the children take turns walking around the circle and tapping heads while the children all sing the tune:

All around the mulberry bush
The monkey chased the weasel
The monkey thought 'twas all in fun
Pop goes the weasel.

When the song gets to "pop goes the weasel," the child who is tapped pops up and chases the tapper as in the other chases. Keep singing and popping until everyone has a turn.

(A variation in case you or the children do not know the song is to play recorded music and pause it periodically. Whoever's head is tapped when the music stops pops up for the chase.)

Let children choose a prize from the prize pot according to how many points they earned, with the highest points going first.

COMMUNITY HELPERS

RECYCLED TOYS FOR THE HOMELESS SHELTER

Category: Creative
Venue: Indoor
Time: 30 minutes
Ages: 8-10
Materials:

- note cards with envelopes (one for each guest and perhaps a few extras in case of do-overs)
- pencils and markers
- wrapping paper
- scissors
- tape
- ribbons and bows
- a variety of thank you gifts (small trinkets from the dollar store) placed in a bag or box

Preparation:
Include in the party invitation the information that each guest should bring a gently used toy from their collection as a donation for children at a local homeless shelter. They should put the toy in a closed bag so as to hide its identity when arriving at the party.

Set up your dining room or kitchen table with enough chairs for each guest. Put the wrapping paper and note materials in the center of the table.

When the guests arrive, take their closed toy bag and place it somewhere out of sight.

Begin the Activity:

Have the children sit on the floor in a circle. Put the bags of toys that the children have brought in the center. The birthday child will begin by picking a bag and taking out the toy. The children then guess who brought it. When the child who brought it has been identified, he or she will tell a little about it and why they thought a child at the homeless shelter would enjoy it.

After the child has told their story, they get to draw a thank-you gift from the bag or box of trinkets. Proceed around the circle until everyone has had a turn.

Then move to the table where the children will wrap their toys and write a short note to the child who will be receiving it. You might need to give them some starter ideas, such as "Hello. My name is _____ and I hope you will enjoy this toy because _____."

Follow up:

Within the next few days, take the birthday child with you to the homeless shelter to deliver the toys. This provides a wonderful life lesson in charity and gratitude.

CRAWLING FOR GIFTS

Category: Active
Venue: Indoor or Outdoor
Time: 15 minutes
Ages: 7-10
Materials:

- A variety of small cardboard boxes (shoe boxes, cereal boxes, ring boxes, shirt boxes, etc.)
- Birthday wrapping paper
- Cellophane tape
- Variety of prizes (1 per guest)
- Blindfold
- Small slips of paper, each with a number starting at one; one slip per guest
- Small paper bag to hold the number slips

Preparation:

Determine the playing area, which should be a large space inside or an outside grassy area. It needs to be large enough for children to crawl around to find a wrapped gift placed within the circle.

Put a prize inside each box, and wrap it. Have the number-slip bag and blindfold handy.

Begin the Activity:

Describe the game to the children. They will each take a turn, blind-folded, to crawl around on the floor to find one of the packages. The other children will give clues to help them find their way to the package; such as "go to the right," "turn around," "go straight ahead," etc. Tell them there is a special gift inside each package, and they will all open them together at the end of the game.

The children sit on the floor or grass in a large circle. You will place the wrapped packages in the middle. With the birthday child going first, each child draws a number slip from the bag to determine the order of their turn.

Whoever has number 1 goes first. They choose a prize box they want to hunt for. You will remove the other boxes and place outside the circle. You then place the blindfold on the hunter and help them get down on their hands and knees. Put the wrapped box somewhere within the circle as far away as possible.

At the signal to begin, the hunter crawls around to find the box. The other children shout out clues. Expect lots of laughter, especially when they crawl into the circle of children by accident.

When they find the box, they take off the blindfold and return to the circle with their gift. Put the gift behind them until all the children have had a turn to find their gift. Proceed with the guest who has the next number to choose a gift to hunt for, and so on. After everyone has been the hunter, they can all open their gifts and discover their prize.

DECORATE THE PARTY

Category: Creative
Venue: Indoor
Time: 15-30 minutes
Ages: 6-8
Materials:

- 1-4 packs of construction paper in various colors
- Scissors
- Glue or paste
- Cellophane tape
- Stapler

Preparation:

For this activity, the guests will make decorations to use at the party. You will need a large table where the children can work together. Put the scissors, glue, tape and stapler in the middle. It will also help to have a sample of each item prepared as a model to show the children. Prepare the construction paper as follows:

For woven placemats: Use regular size construction paper (at least 2 sheets per guests to allow for mistakes and do-overs). Fold each sheet in half with long sides together. Cut slits about one-inch apart from the fold to about one-inch from the edge. Do not cut all the way through.

Cut about 50 one-inch strips of various colored construction paper, the long way. Use two sheets per guest.

For paper chains: Cut several dozen one-inch strips of various colored construction paper, the short way.

For paper lanterns: Use regular size construction paper folded in half the long way.

Begin the Activity:

Tell the children they are going to make decorations to use for the birthday cake time. They will each make their own placemat, as well as paper chains and paper lanterns to decorate the room.

For placemats: Show the children how to weave strips of paper in and out of the slits on the construction paper. They will glue each piece at each end when they finish a row.

For paper chains: Show the children how to make a loop with each strip of paper, gluing or stapling the ends, looping another piece, etc. They can work cooperatively to make longer and longer chains by gluing individual chains together.

For paper lanterns: Show the children how to cut slits starting at the folded side and cutting until about an inch or less from the edge. They can get creative in how close to make their slits. When their slits are all done, they form the paper into a tube and staple the ends together at the top and bottom. Then take a strip of paper to use as a handle, and staple to the top.

Allow about 5 minutes for the children to decorate the room by hanging their lanterns (you may need to help supervise if tape is required) and draping the chains around the chairs and tables. Put their placemats at the birthday cake table. Be sure to take some pictures of their creations. And of course they may take their placemats home (if they are still in good shape).

EDIBLE JEWELRY

Category: Creative

Venue: Indoor

Time: 15 – 30 minutes

Ages: 5-7

Materials:

- 1 box each dried pasta in various shapes with holes (mostaciolli, penne, wagon wheels, etc.)
- 1 box of multi-colored cereal with holes (Cheerios, Froot Loops, etc.)
- Yarn or twine (enough for each child to make two or more necklaces and/or bracelets)
- Magic markers of various colors
- Gift bags (optional)
- Quiet background music (optional)

Preparation:

Prepare a table large enough for the children to sit around. Cover as needed to prevent any magic marker slip-ups. Have some quiet music playing in the background to make the mood more festive.

Put the jewelry materials in the center of the table for the children to share. Cut the yarn or twine into appropriate lengths to make necklaces and bracelets.

Begin the activity:

Show the children how to string the pasta and cereal shapes to make jewelry. They will color the pasta with markers prior to stringing. You can encourage them to make gifts for their family members so that they will take extra care.

You will need to help tie the string when the edible jewelry is complete. They can wear their jewelry for the rest of the party, or put in gift bags to take home.

EGG TOSS SCRAMBLE

Category: Active (and messy)
Venue: Outdoor
Time: 15 minutes
Ages: 8-10
Materials:

- Eggs (4 per guest)
- 1 standard 3 ½ gallon bucket
- 1 large sheet of plywood or similar hard surface area such as a brick wall
- Paper towels for clean up
- Score sheet
- Pencil
- Prizes (1 per guest)

Preparation:

Hard boil half the eggs and refrigerate. The hardboiled eggs and raw eggs need to be the same temperature for the game. Put all the eggs in their cartons, mixing up the hardboiled and raw eggs within each carton.

Set up the plywood target at the end of the yard or driveway. You can also use a wall as a target as long as you don't mind hosing it down later! Have the bucket handy for the second part of the game.

Begin the Activity:

What kid doesn't love making a mess? The object of this game is to guess whether a tossed egg is raw or boiled prior to throwing and discovering the truth. The children will take turns throwing, beginning with the birthday child, lining up according to their birthday months behind the birthday child. The children should stand about 20-30 feet away from the target.

The child steps up to the line and you hand them an egg. They must guess whether it is raw or boiled and announce their prediction to the group. Then they throw the egg at the target and see whether it splats or not. If their guess is correct, they earn a point and go to the end of the line. Continue taking turns until all the eggs are gone.

Now have the children collect the hard boiled eggs from the target area and put them back in the cartons. You should have approximately half the eggs. They will be cracked, but that is OK. You may need to wipe them with paper towels if they need a clean-up.

The next challenge begins with the birthday child, and proceeds taking turns as before. The child stands about three feet from the bucket and tosses a boiled egg into it. Earn a point if successful. Then step back one big step and toss again. Continue tossing and stepping back until there is a miss. Then the next child gets a turn. Score a point for each successful toss.

After everyone has had at least one turn (depending on time), tally up the points. The guests choose a prize from the prize pot according to the number of points earned, highest going first.

FOLLOW-THE-CLUES TREASURE HUNT

Category: Active

Venue: Indoor or Outdoor

Time: 15-30 minutes depending on the number of clues

Ages: 6 – 10 (someone in the group must be able to read simple clues)

Materials:

- Small slips of paper
- Pen or pencil
- Prize items for treasure box
- Box or bag to hold the treasures
- Prizes (1 per guest)

Preparation:

Purchase inexpensive items within your budget from a dollar store that are appropriate for the age group anticipated. For example: rocket balloons, bubble blowers, rubber snakes, rings, candy, etc. Let the birthday child shop with you to select items their friends will enjoy. Purchase enough so that each guest will receive at least one item.

Place items in a small cardboard box or paper bag. You can decorate as you wish, although not necessary. (The kids will be so excited when they find the treasure, they probably will not notice whether it's decorated or not.)

Hide the treasure box or bag somewhere in the house for an indoor party (in a closet, under a bed, inside the clothes dryer, in a dresser drawer, etc.). For an outdoor party, hide somewhere safely within the yard, such as behind a bush or a tree or under lawn furniture.

Prepare the clues. Working backwards, print the clue in legible handwriting or type on small pieces of paper. Fold the paper in half and write the clue number and its location on the back. (This is so you will know where to hide each clue.) Samples are given below. You can prepare your own rhymes for hiding in different locations that you may choose.

Hide the clues. (Do this out of sight of the birthday child prior to the party.) Hide each clue paper so that it will be difficult to find, yet not impossible; for example, tucked under the corner of a rug. You can also tape the clues in out-of-sight spots as needed. Also consider the age of the guests to tailor the level of difficulty. No matter the age level, think of clue locations scattered as far apart as possible. For example, clue #2 in an upstairs bedroom and clue #3 in a basement location. For outdoors, clue #2 in the front yard and clue #3 in the back yard. This will keep the kids moving and extend the time for the activity.

Begin the Activity:
Lay down the ground rules as follows:

1. *You must stay within the boundaries.* If inside, tell them any rooms that are off limits. If outside, define the safe space area, such as not crossing any streets, staying outside of pool fences, or avoiding neighbors' yards.

2. *You must work as a team.* Everyone must have a turn reading a clue. (A guest who is not a reader, or doesn't want to read, may ask for help from a teammate.) Let the birthday child decide the order of who will read before the game begins. Be sure everyone understands when it will be their turn by stating who they will follow. Jack says, "I will read the clue after Ava." And so on.

3. *You must WALK from clue to clue.* Anyone running will get one warning, and then be disqualified.

4. *If and when the treasure is found, the birthday child will distribute the loot.* No grabbing and squabbling allowed.

Give the first clue to the birthday child, who will be the first designated reader. He or she will read the clue out loud. The team solves the clue together, and then proceeds (walking) to the location of the next clue. (A parent or another adult will need to monitor as rule keeper.) All the teammates search the area until someone finds the hidden clue.

Proceed taking turns reading the clues out loud until the treasure is found. The birthday child will distribute the gifts, being sure that everyone gets an equal share of the loot.

Sample clues for an indoor treasure hunt

In this example, you will hide the treasure in a bedroom closet. You draw a blank line for the answer as shown in the sample. We've provided the answer just so you don't even have to think. See, we told you this book would simplify your life.

Front of paper
1. (Given to birthday child to begin.)
    Back of paper
    When you're tired
    You rest your head.
    Find the first clue
    Under mommy's_____. (bed)

2. (Under mommy's bed)
    The next clue
    Is not too far.
    Go to the place
    Where you keep a _____. (car)

3. (Garage)
    Do you like
    The color pink?
    The next clue

Is in a bathroom_____. (sink)

4. (Sink) Which bathroom sink? … you decide.
    Some kids may think
    This game's not fair.
    Look for the next clue
    Under a _____. (chair)

5. (Chair) Which chair? … you decide.
    Do you have a
    Secret club?
    The next clue is
    Near the bath_____. (tub)

6. (Bathtub). Which bathtub? … you decide.
    You are a
    Very good guesser.
    Find the next clue
    Behind a clothes_____. (dresser)

7. (Dresser). Which dresser? … you decide.
    Don't be scared of
    A little bug.
    The next clue is located
    Under a _____. (rug)

8. (Rug). Which rug? … you decide.
    This is becoming
    Quite a chase.
    Look for the next clue
    In a wood book_____. (case)

9. (Bookcase). Which bookcase? … you decide.
    One thing that

I know for certain.
The next clue is hiding
Behind a _____. (curtain)

10. (Curtain). Which curtain? ... you decide.
You have made a
Large deposit.
You will now find the treasure
In a bedroom _____. (closet)

Sample clues for an outdoor treasure hunt. In this example, the treasure will be hidden under a bush, covered with leaves.

1. (Given to birthday child to begin)
Few things in life
Are ever free.
Find the first clue
Near a very tall _____. (tree)

2. (Tall tree)
Your team is
Clever as a fox.
Find the next clue
Inside the mail_____. (box)

3. (Mailbox)
You can count
One, two, three, four.
Now go look
Near the back_____. (door)

4. (Backdoor)
To tell the time
You need a clock.

Now go look in front
Under a _____. (rock)

5. (front yard rock)
    Please keep silent,
    Please don't talk.
    Look for the next clue
    Near the side_____. (walk)

6. (sidewalk)
    Do not run
    And do not push.
    The treasure is buried
    Under a _____. (bush) You might give a hint as to where the
    bush is located, or let them search the entire yard as time permits.

FOOD CHALLENGE RELAYS

Category: Action

Venue: Indoor

Time: 15 minutes

Ages: 8-10

Materials:

- Masking tape to mark a start and finish line
- Hard boiled eggs (1 per guest)
- 2 large lemons
- 2 pencils
- Large box of raisins
- Toothpicks (1 per guest)
- 2 saucers
- Score sheet and pencil
- Prizes (1 per guest)

Preparation:

Determine the playing area, which should be a large carpeted room or hard surface where the children can safely crawl. Move furniture to the side. Use the masking tape to mark a starting line, and a finish line on the opposite side of the room. You can also mark a line for each team from start to finish which they have to follow. Have the materials handy.

Begin the Activity:

There are three parts to this game. First, have the children count off by two's to form two teams. The birthday child is captain of one team, and the child with the closest birthday is captain of the other team. In case of an odd number of children, the birthday child will be on the team with one fewer players and will get two turns. You will scramble the teams for each activity so that the children compete against different players.

The captains stand behind the starting line, about 10 feet from each other. The other players form a line behind their captain.

The first challenge is to roll a boiled egg with your nose down the line from start to finish. Give every child a boiled egg. On your signal, the first players crawl to the finish line pushing the egg. When they reach the finish line, the next child on their team starts, and so on. The team to reach the finish line first gets a point scored for each player on the team.

For the second challenge, scramble the teams who compete to roll a lemon from start to finish and back by crawling down the line pushing the lemon with a pencil. The children line up in order making two lines behind their number one player. Put a lemon and a pencil at the start of each line. On your command, the first two challengers start for the finish line, rolling their lemon down the line with the pencil. They may not touch the lemon with their hand or anything other than the pencil. If so, they must return to start and go to the end of the line.

They touch the finish line, turn around, and go back to the start line. The first to arrive scores a point. When both players have returned to the start line, the second two challengers take the lemon and pencil and begin on your command, and so on until each pair has had a turn.

For the third challenge, form two new teams by counting off as before. The birthday child captains one team, and the child with the furthest birthday is captain of the other. Have the children form two long lines that stretch from the start line to the finish line. They will be at least an arm's length from each other.

Give every child a toothpick. Give each captain a saucer filled with raisins. There must be at least 5-10 raisins per guest, allowing for some spillage. The object is to be the first team for all players to spear and eat four raisins each.

On your command, the captain carries the saucer of raisins to the next in line on their team. That child must spear four raisins at once onto the toothpick (no touching with fingers, only using the toothpick) and eat the four from the toothpick. Violating the touching rule means they must spear an extra raisin for each touch.

Then the captain carries the saucer to the next in line who spears and eats as before. At the finish line the captain is the last to spear and eat four raisins. The first team to finish the challenge scores a point for each team member.

Award prizes according to the number of points scored, with the child with the most points choosing first from the prize pot.

FOOT RACE RELAYS

Category: Active

Venue: Outdoor

Time: 15-30 minutes

Ages: 8-10

Materials:

- 2 plastic laundry baskets
- 2 pairs of adult-size socks
- 2 pairs of large-size adult shoes
- Rope or string for starting line
- Prizes (1 per guest)

Preparation:

Set up a large grassy area for the relay races. Be sure there are no impediments to safety since children will be doing some of these races barefoot or in socks. Lay down a starting line. Opposite the starting line as far away as possible, place each of the laundry baskets a short distance from each other. Put one pair of socks and one pair of shoes in each basket.

Begin the Activity:

Have the children count by two's to form two teams. The birthday child will be the captain of one team, and the child with the birthday closest will captain the other team. The children form two lines behind each captain. There are three parts to this foot race relay. Explain each in turn.

Shoe mix-up relay

Have all the children take off their shoes. You will take all the shoes and place each team's shoes in the basket opposite their line. Mix them up.

On the start signal, the first player runs to the basket, finds their own shoes and puts them on. Then run back to their team line, and the next player takes off. The first team to have all players return to the line with their own shoes is the winner and gets a point for round one.

Sock relay

Round two begins with each team taking turns to run to the basket, take off their shoes, put the adult socks on, take off the socks and put their shoes back on, and run back to the team. The next player takes off to repeat the task, until one team is declared the winner.

Shoe relay

For the final challenge, the children will take turns running to the basket, taking off their shoes and putting on the adult shoes. They then must get back to their team wearing the adult shoes and then go back to the basket to put the adult shoes back in. They put their own shoes back on and return to the team line. The team to complete the task first is the winner.

The children then choose prizes based upon the number of points their team earned. If one team did not get any points, they will choose last for consolation prizes.

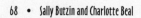

FOUR SQUARE

Category: Active
Venue: Outdoor
Time: 15-30 minutes
Ages: 8-10
Materials:

- Chalk or colored tape to mark the playing court
- Rubber playground ball or other large bouncing ball
- Score sheet and pencil
- Prizes (1 per guest)

Preparation:
This game is played on a hard surface such as a driveway or patio where the ball will bounce. Mark off the court with chalk or tape in a four square grid. The total court is a 16 foot square, marked off into four 8 foot squares. Write the numeral 1 on one of the squares ; the square diagonally is marked with numeral 4. The other two squares will be numeral 2 and 3. Mark an *on deck* line. (Note that some courts are marked with A,B,C,D instead of with numerals.)

Begin the Activity:
Have the children line up according to birthday months, with the birthday child going first. The birthday child goes to Square 4 and the next three children go to a subsequent square. They stand outside the corner of their square. The other children wait their turn on the *on deck* line.

The object of the game is to advance to square number 4 by eliminating other players. The players bounce the ball to each other until someone creates a fault, such as hitting an outside line or going out of bounds. The player with the fault goes to the back of the on-deck line and the other players advance to the next higher number. A new player from the on-deck line goes to Square 1.

Here are examples of faults:

- Failing to hit the ball into another square;
- Allowing the ball to bounce more than once in their own square;
- Hitting the ball out of bounds or onto an inside line;
- Hitting the ball incorrectly, such as holding, catching or carrying;
- Hitting the ball with a part of the body that is not hands;
- Hitting the ball out of turn (poaching).

The child in Square 4 is the server and starts the game by bouncing it to any other square. The server gets two chances to get it in a square correctly before being moved back to the on-deck line. The other children must bounce the ball correctly to another square when it hits their square. They can move around outside or inside their own box as needed to get to their ball. Keep bouncing from square to square until someone commits a fault. That child goes to the back of the on-deck line, and the next in line goes to Square 1. The others move up to the next square in sequence.

Consider limiting the number of turns a child can stay in Square 4 in case one child seems to be dominating the game.

Score the game by awarding a point to any child who reaches Square 4. (The birthday child gets an automatic point by being the first to go to Square 4.) The game should proceed quickly with a lot of in-and-out activity so that everyone has multiple chances to advance to Square 4.

When time expires, guests can choose a prize according to the score sheet, highest points going first.

GUESSING GAMES

Category: Quiet Games (Time Fillers)
Venue: Indoor
Time: 15 minutes
Ages: 5-10
Materials:

- Large bags of hard candies (such as M&M's or Skittles—enough to fill several jars)
- 3-5 glass jars (of various sizes) with lids
- Small slips of paper to write guesses
- Pencils
- Score sheet
- Hand sanitizer
- Sandwich size zipper bags (one per guest)
- Paper towels or paper plates (one per guest) to use as sorting mats
- Prize (one special prize; everyone will get a bag of candies as prizes)

Preparation:
Fill each jar nearly to the top with candies and screw on the tops. For the largest and final jar, you should pre-count the candies and write down the number so you will remember. This will save time later. Have the guessing paper slips, pencils, plastic bags, and sorting mats available.

Begin the Activity:
Have the children sit around a large table or in a circle on the floor. Give everyone a squirt of hand sanitizer. Tell the children they are going to estimate (guess) how many candies are in each jar. Start by giving the smallest jar to the birthday child, who will look at it for a few seconds, shake it, and pass to the next child. After each child handles the jar, they write their estimate on a slip of paper with their name on it, fold it, and put it back in the center.

After everyone has written their estimate, open the jar and hand it to the first child, who will count out ten candies and put them in front of him on a sorting mat, and pass to the next child to count out ten. Continue until all the candies are out of the jar. Have the children then count by ten's (a good math skill by the way) to determine how many candies were in the jar. Open the estimates. Anyone within 10-20 (or any amount you determine depending on the ages) gets a point.

The children will put the candies in their plastic bag, and get ready for the next round. You may let them eat a few as well.

On the first round, most estimates will be wildly off track, especially for the younger children. Hopefully they will get more accurate as the game proceeds. (Another good math skill.)

Proceed with the second jar of candies as before. Be sure to have the children compare this new jar to the one they just opened. Hopefully their estimates will be more accurate. Score points as before.

If you find that passing the jar and counting ten at a time is taking too long, you can pour a handful from the jar onto each paper towel and have each child sort theirs in groups of ten. Leftovers go back in the jar and added to the final tally.

For the final jar, if time is running short, you can have the children write their estimates and then you will verify the total based on your count when you prepared the jars.

For a variation (and more math skills), on the last jar, have everyone eat one candy. Who can tell how many are now in the jar? Eat two candies. Now how many? And so on. Score points for correct answers.

Whoever has the most points will win the grand prize. All the children keep their candy bags to take home.

HOPSCOTCH

Category: Active (Time Filler)
Venue: Outdoor
Time: 15 minutes
Ages: 5-10
Materials:
- Chalk
- 1 small stone (about the size of a golf ball)
- Prizes (1 per guest)

Preparation:
This ageless game requires little preparation, making it a good time filler. You will need a sidewalk or driveway to draw the hopscotch grid. We are assuming everyone knows how to do this, but just in case, you will draw boxes in single and double patterns. Write a large numeral in each box. Depending on the children's ages, there can be five boxes or as many as a dozen.

Begin the Activity:
The children line up behind the first box on the hopscotch grid. The birthday child goes first. The others form a line behind alphabetically by first name. The object is to hop on one foot (two if you are on a double box set) to all the boxes in numerical order and back again without touching a line, or touching the box with the stone on it.

The child throws the stone to box one, and then hops to the last box and back, remembering not to step on the box with the stone. On the way back, they pick up the stone without stepping in the box, and hop back to the start. If successful, throw the stone to box two, and continue as before. A throw that touches a line is OK. Keep going until they either step on a line, use two feet in a single box, fail to pick up the stone, or fail to land the stone in the correct box when throwing it. Then return to the back of the line and the next child gets a turn.

When each child's turn comes up again, they throw the stone to the next consecutive numbered box from the one they completed on their last turn. This gets more difficult as the boxes get increasingly farther away. It may take several turns to get the stone to land in the box. You might consider giving them three throws before they have to go to the back of the line.

At the end of the game, children pick prizes from the prize pot according to the order of who got to the farthest numbered box and back successfully. In case of ties, you can have a *toss-off* to see who can throw the stone in sequence the farthest without missing.

HOT AND COLD

Category: Quiet games (time filler)
Venue: Indoor
Time: 15 minutes
Ages: 5-10
Materials:

- Prizes (at least 1 for each guest)

Preparation:

Easy. This requires no preparation, other than to get a room cleaned up for the guests to sit.

Begin the activity:

The birthday child gets the first turn as the seeker. The seeker leaves the room and goes into another room with the door closed. You might send another guest with the seeker to be sure there is no peaking or listening.

In the meantime, the remaining guests pick an object in the room for the seeker to find. When the seeker returns, he goes to the middle of the room and turns around three times. Then the hunt begins.

The guests give hints by saying "hot," "warm," "cold," "colder," etc. as the seeker moves around the room looking for the object. When the seeker finally identifies the object, they win a prize and choose the next guest to leave the room and become the seeker.

Continue until everyone has had at least one turn.

HUNTING FOR KISSES

Category: Active

Venue: Outdoor or Indoor

Time: 15 minutes

Ages: 5-7

Materials:

- Several large bags of candy kisses (or other wrapped candies)
- Collection bags
- Kitchen timer
- Prizes (1 per guest)

Preparation:

This activity is similar to an Easter egg hunt. Determine the boundaries within your yard or inside where the hunt will take place. Hide the candy kisses in a variety of places, some easy and some harder to find. The more candy you hide, the longer the activity will take.

Note that if it is a hot day, you should use wrapped hard candies that will not melt.

Begin the Activity:

Give each child a collection bag. Show them where the boundaries are for the hunt. Determine a reasonable time, probably 5-10 minutes, and set the timer. Off they go.

When time is up, they bring their collection bags back to home base. They each count how many kisses they found. Starting with the child with the most collected, they take turns choosing a prize from the prize pot. And of course they keep the kisses that they found to take home.

ICE CUBE RELAY

Category: Active

Venue: Outdoor

Time: 15 -30 minutes depending on the number of guests

Ages: 5-10

Materials:

- 2 table forks
- Small bowl of ice cubes
- Prizes (1 per guest)
- Rope or string for a starting line

Preparation:

Set up two obstacle courses with a chair or other object at the end as the goal. Depending upon the ages of the children, the goal should be far away for older kids (8-10), and not so far for younger guests (5-7). Place some obstacles along the way toward the goal such as a small wastebasket to step over and a step ladder to crawl under. Each course should be identical. Again, consider the ages of the guests as to the difficulty of the obstacles.

Use a rope or string on the ground as the starting line.

Begin the Activity:

Have the children number off in two's to form two teams. The teams form two lines behind the starting line facing the goals. The birthday child is the leader for one team, and whoever's birthday is closest to the birthday child is the leader for the other team. The children line up one behind the other behind the leader.

Give a fork and ice cube to each leader. Give the "ready, set, go" command. The children must balance the ice cube on the fork while proceeding to the goal, maneuvering any obstacles along the way. When they reach the goal, they must go around the chair and then proceed back to their team, also maneuvering the obstacles on the way back.

If they drop the ice cube, they may pick it up and keep going. (For older children, you may require that they use only the fork to pick it up, for a little more challenge.)

When they return to the team, they hand the fork and ice cube to the next in line, and return to the back of the line. The next child proceeds to the goal and around the obstacles as before. Be sure to have an ample supply of ice cubes so that each child starts with a fresh ice cube.

The first team to get everyone back to the line with the original leader in front is the winner. Everyone on the team gets a prize.

For the other team, let any remaining guests complete the activity for a consolation prize. Make the winning prizes a little nicer than the consolation prizes, so the winners have bragging rights.

Variations for more challenges for older children
- Balance the ice cube on a table knife;
- Balance uncooked eggs on a fork;
- Hold the ice cube between your teeth.

KEEP AWAY

Category: Active
Venue: Outdoor
Time: 15 minutes
Ages: 8-10
Materials:

- Large ball such as a soccer ball, football, or rubber playground ball
- Score sheet and pencil
- Prizes (1 per guest)

Preparation:
Determine the playing field, which should be a large grassy area or similar open space. There is no other preparation required.

Begin the Activity:
Have the children form a large circle, with the birthday child in the middle. Depending on ages, the circle should be large enough to toss the ball around with some difficulty, but not impossible. During the game you can have the children each step back if it seems the circle is too small.

The object of the game is for the child in the middle of the circle to intercept the ball as the children in the circle toss it back and forth, trying to keep it away from the child in the middle. When the middle child is successful in intercepting, they change places with the child who last tossed the ball. That child goes to the middle of the circle, and the game proceeds until everyone has had at least one turn in the middle. The toss must be to a child across the circle, not to someone standing next to the tosser.

To keep the game moving, have a rule that the children must throw the ball within 3 seconds. Have a penalty for throwing it beyond the circle of children. The child who threw it over must go to the center. Also if the child in the circle does not catch the ball, they must go to the middle.

Keep score by giving a point for a child every time they intercept the toss. Award prizes by letting guests select a prize from the prize pot according to points earned.

KICK THE CAN

Category: Active
Venue: Outdoor
Time: 15-30 minutes
Ages: 5-10
Materials:

- Prizes (at least 1 per guest)
- 2 empty tin cans with the labels removed
- Small slips of paper to write guests' names
- Score sheet and pencil
- Kitchen timer

Preparation:

This classic game is always fun for children of all ages. We have adapted the rules for Best Buddies Birthdays so everyone stays involved. The game works best in a very large space with trees to run around and hide.

Write each guest's name on a small slip of paper and place in one of the empty cans.

Begin the Activity:

Place the cans in the middle of the playing field. All the children stand in a circle around the cans. Let the birthday child be the first "tagger." The tagger stays put, closes his eyes and slowly counts out loud to ten, while the other children run and hide somewhere within the boundaries of the playing field.

The tagger then takes a slip of paper out of the name can and calls out the name. (You will hold the can with the names.) He then tries to find and tag that child. The one who is about to be tagged must take off running toward the can and kick the can before being tagged. If he successfully kicks the can before being tagged, he gets one point. If he gets tagged before kicking the can, he becomes the next tagger and the tagger gets the point. You will need to keep the score sheet and the penalty box timer (see rules for penalties below).

After each can-kicking episode, the children return to the circle and go hide again in another place. The name slip goes back in the name can so all the names are always available for picking each time. The same name can only be picked up to three times to keep everyone involved.

Continue the game until everyone has at least one point. The children can select prizes in turn according to who has the most points.

Rules:
1. Everyone must have a turn to be the tagger.
2. You cannot pursue the same child more than three times. (This assures that a slow child does not always get picked on.)
3. No pushing or knocking anyone down. You will receive a two-minute penalty time out if this happens.
4. Stay within the boundaries of the playing area.

KICKBALL BASEBALL

Category: Active

Venue: Outdoor

Time: 30 minutes

Ages: 8-10

Materials:

- Rubber kickball (large ball that will not hurt a player being hit)
- 4 small plywood boards or similar to serve as bases and home plate
- Poster board and markers for a scoreboard
- Prizes (1 per guest)

Preparation:

You need a large grassy area for this game. Set up as a baseball diamond with a home plate and three bases. Determine the boundaries for fouls and home runs.

Begin the Activity:

Divide the guests into two teams by counting off. Any team with an odd number and fewer players will get an extra out. The team with the birthday child will go to bat first. The other team goes to the field to cover the bases and outfield. The children can decide who will pitch first and which positions to play. After each inning they must switch positions, and everyone must pitch at least once.

The game is played like baseball. You will be the umpire at home plate. The pitcher rolls the ball to the batter who kicks it out to the field. The fielders must catch the ball and then throw the ball to try to hit the runner with the ball before he or she reaches the next base or home plate. Players who get hit are out. Players who get to a base are safe. Players who cross home plate earn a point for the team.

Three strikes (missed kicks) and the player is out. A ball kicked out of bounds will also be considered a strike. Three outs and the team is out, exchanging places with the fielding team.

Play at least three innings, or until time runs out. The team with the most points gets first choice of the prize pot. The other team picks last.

LOCKS AND KEYS

Category: Quiet games
Venue: Indoor
Time: 15 minutes
Ages: 5-7
Materials:

- A variety of small padlocks with keys (1 per guest)
- Pillow case or large cloth bag
- Prizes (1 per guest)

Preparation:

Check to be sure that each lock has a key. Lock each padlock and place the keys in a separate place to pass out later. Place the locked padlocks inside the pillowcase or bag.

Begin the Activity:

There is something fascinating to children about locks and keys. Have the children sit in a circle on the floor. Place the bag of locks in the center. Give each child a key.

The game begins with the birthday child going first by reaching into the bag without looking inside, and taking out a lock. Try to open it with the key. Does it open? If not, the lock goes back in the bag and the child sitting to the birthday child's left takes a turn. If it unlocks, the child keeps the lock and key. They can play with it as the game proceeds.

Proceed taking turns until all the locks with matching keys have been retrieved. If there is still time, retrieve all the keys, put the locks in the bag, and start another round.

At the end of the game, everyone picks a prize from the prize pot, starting with the child who found the first matching lock and key. Each child also gets to keep their lock and key to take home.

MAGIC TRICKS

Category: Quiet Games
Venue: Indoor
Time: 30 minutes
Ages: 8-10
Materials:

- Prizes (1 per guest)
- Medium size balloons (at least 2 or 3 per guest)
- 1 tube of lip balm
- Thin wooden skewers with a sharp point or long round toothpicks (1 per guest)

Preparation:

Magic tricks are a great way for the birthday child to shine in front of his or her friends. You will teach the tricks to your child a few days prior to the guests arriving. It is a good idea to have a couple of practice sessions on the day of the party to avoid any embarrassment.

Black Magic

The trick is that the magician will guess an item that has been chosen while not seeing it. The guests sit together in the living room or family room. You will serve as the magician's assistant. The magician leaves the room and goes into another room and shuts the door. Send a guest to be sure the door is closed and the magician cannot hear. Meanwhile the remaining guests choose an object in the room for the magician to guess.

When the magician returns, you will begin pointing to items in the room and ask "Is this it?" The magician will answer "no" until you point to any object that is black. That will also be a "no." The trick is that the item you point to AFTER the black item will be the one picked by the guests. "Is it this?" and now the answer is "yes!"

Do the trick a few more times, and then ask if anyone has figured out the trick. If someone thinks they have, send them out of the room and let them try. Finally, let the birthday magician reveal the trick so their friends can try it at home.

This and That

This trick is a variation on Black Magic. The trick is that you keep pointing to objects that have not been picked and say, "Is it this?" The answer is "no." But when you point to the correct object you say, "Is it THAT?" The answer is "yes."

As before, let some guests try it if they think they know the trick before the birthday magician reveals the magic.

One Finger; Two Fingers

Another variation is for the accomplice to touch items with one finger and ask, "Is this it?" The answer is "no." Then point to the chosen object with two fingers and ask, "Is this it?" The answer is "yes."

Pierce the Balloon

This trick will amaze the guests, and they will have fun learning it to show off at home. The trick is to coat the tip of a wooden skewer or toothpick with lip balm. Be sure to do this out of sight of the guests.

Blow up a balloon and tie it. You can ask the guests to help if they are able. The birthday magician will say, "I have magic powers to poke this balloon and it will not pop!" Do they believe it? Of course the guests think it is impossible.

Begin by gently twisting the coated tip into the thickest part of the balloon (the point opposite the tied opening) until the point breaks through the skin. You should also be able to push a skewer all the way through and out the other side of the balloon if it is long enough. Amazing.

Then have the birthday child teach the trick to the guests and let them practice with their own balloon and coated toothpick or skewer. Provide several balloons for each guest in case there are a few pops until they master the trick.

You can provide a prize for each guest who masters the trick. Also provide some extra balloons and a skewer for them to take home to show off to their family and friends.

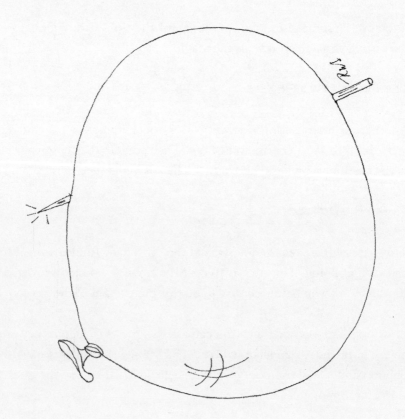

MAKE ME LAUGH

Category: Quiet Games
Venue: Indoor
Time: 15 minutes
Ages: 8-10
Materials:

- Empty picture frame (about 16"x20")
- Kitchen chair or similar
- Kitchen timer
- Score sheet and pencil
- Prizes (1 per guest)

Preparation:
Gather the materials. Take the glass out of the picture frame.

Begin the Activity:
The object of the game is to score the best time for not laughing when it is your turn to sit in the picture frame. There are group challenges and individual challenges.

The children sit on the floor or on chairs in a line side by side. Place the kitchen chair opposite and facing the line of children, about ten feet or so away. Starting with the birthday child, the children will take turns sitting in the chair and holding the picture frame up to their face. The children can go in order of their birthdays closest to the birthday child.

The child in the chair holds up the picture frame and assumes a serious pose, looking toward the line of children. On your command, you start the timer, and the other children try to make the child with the frame laugh. They can make funny faces, say funny things, or stand in place and make silly motions. They may not advance any closer, but must stay in place in the line.

When the child finally laughs, stop the timer and write the time on the score sheet. The next child goes to the facing chair, holds up the picture frame, and the game continues until everyone has had a turn.

The next round is an individual challenge. Taking turns being the frame holder and the challenger, the challenger says, "I bet I can make you laugh in _____ seconds." Start the timer and the challenger begins silly antics to make the framed child laugh. If the challenger makes the other laugh within the timeframe they stated, he gets a bonus point added to his score sheet. If the framed child does not laugh within the challenge time, she gets a bonus point added.

Continue until everyone has had a turn in the frame and to be the challenger. Tally up the points. The guests choose a prize from the prize pot in order of score, highest points being first.

MEMORY GAMES

Category: Quiet games (time filler)
Venue: Indoor or outdoor
Time: 15 minutes
Ages: 8-10
Materials:

- Prizes (at least 1 per guest)

Begin the Activity:
Have the children sit on the floor in a circle. Choose a category such as a grocery store. The birthday child will begin by saying, "I went to the grocery store and I bought Apples" (or something that begins with A from a grocery store). The child seated to the left says, "I went to the grocery store and I bought Apples and Bananas" (or something that begins with B).

The game proceeds around the circle with each child repeating what has already been said and adding an item according to the next letter in the alphabet.

The object is to get around the circle and back to the birthday child with no mistakes. On the first round, everyone gets a prize if they make it. Then challenge the guests to make it two times around the circle; three times, etc. Award prizes for each challenge accomplished. Children can help one another as needed. Make it a cooperative game so no one gets embarrassed.

Variations

"I went to the zoo and saw an Alligator, Bat, etc."

"I went to the circus and saw an Acrobat, Balloon, etc."

"I went to a restaurant and ate an Apple Pie, Bread, etc."

MOTHER MAY I?

Category: Active
Venue: Outdoor is best, but it can be done indoors in a large room
Time: 15 minutes
Ages: 5-7
Materials:

- Prizes (1 per guest)
- Rubber bands for bracelets
- Masking tape or string to make a starting line

Preparation:
This is a time-honored game that young children have enjoyed for generations. It meets their need to be "mother" and be in charge.

Determine the playing field, which should be a large grassy area or a room with furniture cleared away to the side. Set up a starting line.

Begin the activity:
The birthday child will be the first mother. In the case of boys, you can interchange with father.

The other children make a line shoulder to shoulder behind the starting line on the opposite side of the playing field. The mother stands on the opposite side facing the children.

Mother begins to make commands, such as "walk two baby steps" or "jump backwards one jump." The other children must say, "Mother may I?" and mother must respond, "Yes you may," before they can move to the command. Any child who forgets to say, "Mother may I?" must return back to the starting line.

All movements should advance toward the mother. In other words, if the command is to "walk backwards," the children will turn around and walk backwards toward the mother. This keeps the game moving along.

The object is to be the first child to get across the field and touch mother. After a few tries, the children will soon learn to take as big steps as possible to be first, and mother will figure out commands to keep them at bay. Mother can also step up the pace of commands to make some children forget to say, "Mother may I?" and have to go back to the starting line. Mother can only give forward commands, but can vary whether they are giant steps, baby steps, how many steps, etc.

The first child to reach and tap mother becomes the next mother to give commands. That child also gets a rubber band bracelet to use when collecting prizes. Make a rule that no one child can collect more than three bracelets as the game continues. Try to make sure that every guest earns at least one bracelet.

Children will select from the prize pot according to how many bracelets they have earned.

Variation

Each child along the line will determine what they want to do and ask mother for permission. In other words, Lori may ask, "Mother, may I take three giant steps?" Mother may say, "yes" or "no," but only two times for "no." This variation encourages a little strategy for the kids to figure out how to get to mother on their own.

MUSICAL MYSTERY SACK

Category: Quiet Games
Venue: Indoor
Time: 15 minutes
Ages: 5-10
Materials:

- CD player and CD of children's songs (or music the birthday child enjoys)
- A variety of prizes (1 per guest)
- Small gift boxes of various sizes (1 per guest)
- A variety of wrapping paper
- Cellophane tape
- Pillow case

Preparation:
Place a prize in each of the boxes. Wrap each box in 3-5 layers of varied wrapping paper. Place the CD player, music CD, and pillow case near the game area.

Begin the Activity:
The children sit on the floor in a circle. Put the wrapped prize boxes and the pillow case in the middle of the circle. There are two parts to this game.

The first part begins with the birthday child choosing a wrapped package from the center. Then start the music and the guests begin to pass the gift from child to child. Stop the music. The child holding the package when the music stops will unwrap the first layer of wrapping paper. Be sure to instruct them to do it gently so the next layer is revealed.

The music starts again and the children pass the package along until the music stops again. The child holding the package unwraps the next layer, and so on until the prize is completely unwrapped. Then the prize goes into the pillowcase. The game proceeds until all the packages have been unwrapped and all are inside the pillowcase.

Now the second part begins. Take some of the discarded wrapping paper and wad it into a ball. Secure with tape.

The birthday child gets the paper ball first. Start the music and the children pass the ball along from child to child. Stop the music. Whoever has the ball when the music stops gets to pull a prize from the pillowcase, without looking. They can feel inside it to try to retrieve something they remember from the first part of the game. Continue passing the ball to the music, and stopping periodically for someone holding the ball to retrieve a prize.

If a child does not like the prize they retrieved, they can put it back and wait for another turn. But they only get one chance to put a prize back. On the second draw, they must keep that prize.

Continue the game until everyone has a prize.

MUSICAL SINGING GAMES

Category: Quiet games (time filler)
Venue: Indoor or Outdoor
Time: 15 minutes
Ages: 5-7
Materials:

- Prizes (at least 1 per guest)
- Recorded music (optional)

Preparation:
Musical games are always fun for the younger children. There is little preparation. Just set aside ample space where the children can move about freely. Tell the children that everyone who joins in and sings clearly without shouting or acting silly will win a participation prize.

Begin the Activity:
You will lead the children in some classic children's action songs. The birthday child may know of others learned at school. If you are unfamiliar with these songs, the full lyrics, music and actions are available on the Internet.

Hokey Pokey

(This is a dance performed while standing in a circle.)

You put your right hand in
Your put your right hand out
You put your right hand in
And you shake it all about
You do the Hokey Pokey
And you turn yourself around
That's what it's all about. (Clap, clap)

Continue with left hand; right foot; left foot; head; backside; whole self.

Who Stole the Cookies?

(This is a chant sung while sitting in a circle.)

Who stole the cookies from the cookie jar? (All the children say this.)
_____ stole the cookies from the cookie jar. (You name the birth-day child first.)
Who me? (says the child who was named)
Yes you! (say all the kids)
Couldn't be. (says the child named)
Then who? (say all the kids)
_____ stole the cookies from the cookie jar. (The child names another kid in the circle; continue the chant until everyone has been named at least once)

Ring Around the Rosie

(The children sing holding hands and marching around in a circle; and then all fall down on command. Get up and continue for a few more rounds until the laughter dies down.)

Ring around the rosie
A pocket full of posies
Ashes, ashes
All fall down.

Head, Shoulders, Knees and Toes

(Children touch the body part when named. Each round gets faster and faster until they can't keep up.)

Head, shoulders, knees and toes
Knees and toes

Head, shoulders, knees and toes
Knees and toes
Head, shoulders,
Knees and toes
Head, shoulders, knees and toes
Knees and toes.

If You're Happy and You Know It

If you're happy and you know it
Clap your hands (clap, clap)
If you're happy and you know it
Clap your hands (clap, clap)
If you're happy and you know it
Then your face will surely show it
If you're happy and you know it
Clap your hands (clap, clap)
Each round adds something else to touch or do:
Pat your head; touch your nose; pull your ears; etc.

To add a challenge, say "do all three" after each third verse. (clap, clap; touch, touch; pull, pull)

Bingo

(At each spelling of Bingo, children clap instead of saying the letter, until the last verse is all claps.)

There was a farmer had a dog
And Bingo was his name-oh
B-I-N-G-O
B-I-N-G-O
B-I-N-G-O
And Bingo was his name-oh.

NASTY BEANS

(PASS THE BEACH BALL)

Category: Quiet Games
Venue: Indoor or Outdoor
Time: 15 minutes
Ages: 5-7
Materials:
- Prizes (1 per guest)
- Beach ball or similar
- CD player with children's music loaded
- 1 bag of dry beans
- Small plastic cups (optional)

Preparation:
Choose music that the birthday child enjoys. Place the CD player in the area where the activity will take place. Have a supply of dry beans handy. Provide plastic cups if some guests do not have pockets.

Begin the activity:
The children stand in a circle, at least 3 feet apart. Tell them the rules of the game: pass the ball to the person next to them and keep passing while the music plays. When the music stops, the child holding the ball gets a *nasty bean*. This is not good. The object is to get the fewest number of nasty beans.

Start the music and start the game. The birthday child begins passing the ball. You will periodically pause the music, and give a "nasty bean" to the child holding the ball. They can put the beans in their pocket or in a small plastic cup if they do not have a pocket.

Keep playing until everyone has at least one bean, or as long as the children are enjoying the game. At the end, have them count their nasty beans and select a prize, starting with the child who has the fewest beans.

OBSTACLE COURSE CHALLENGES

Category: Active
Venue: Outdoor
Time: 15 minutes
Ages: 5-7
Materials:

- A variety of prizes (1 per guest)
- Score sheet and pencil

Preparation:
Survey your yard to determine obstacles that can become the challenge courses (trees, picnic table, swing set, fence posts, etc). You will use your imagination and creativity to set up challenges for the children to navigate, with the difficulty depending on the children's ages.

Begin the Activity:
The children will count off to determine the order of play, with the birthday child going first. After you have set up a few challenges, you can let the children determine some new challenge courses. They often come up with some doozeys.

To keep everyone involved while they wait their turn, you can assign the waiting children to stand at an obstacle to be sure that the runner completes it successfully. For example, if the challenge is to run around a tree three times, the child watching the station will count to three. At the end of each run, the children all move forward to the next station, while the child at the last station rotates to the starting line to be the next runner.

Here are some examples of obstacle course challenges.
1. Run to the fence and touch it; run to the swing set and run around it two times; run back to the fence and tap it two times; run back to home base and slap my hand.

2. Run to the picnic bench and walk across it; jump down and run to the garbage can and run around it three times; walk backwards to the fence; turn around and run back to home base and slap my hand.

3. Run to the driveway and tiptoe across it; run back across and tap the garage door; run to the pine tree and kick it; run back to home base and slap my hand.

4. Run to the garbage can and go around it two times; hop to the tallest tree and tap it three times; walk backwards to the sign post and touch it with your back; run back to home base and slap my hand.

Begin each challenge by demonstrating the course and what they need to do at each stopping point. Then ask each child when it is their turn, "I challenge you to complete the course in 15 seconds. Can you do it?" They also have the option of requesting more time if they think they need it, or less time if they are the braggadocio type. But the challenge is to beat the designated time, and to be the player to complete the course correctly in the least amount of time.

Say "Ready, set, go," and the first player takes off. All the other children count aloud with you, "One second, two seconds, three seconds, etc." loudly so that the runner can hear. If the runner gets back on or before the challenge time, they get a point. At the end of each challenge course, the player who completed it in the fewest number of seconds gets a bonus point.

When all the challenges have been completed, tally the points. The children can select from the prize pot in the order of points earned.

POPCORN BINGO

Category: Quiet games
Venue: Indoor
Time: 15-30 minutes
Ages: 5-10
Materials:

- Prizes (1 per guest)
- Bingo game
- Popcorn
- Small bowls that hold about one cup (1 per player)
- Score sheet and pencil

Preparation:

Purchase an inexpensive Bingo game. For younger children there are variations where the squares are easier to find. Pop and season enough popcorn for all the guests to have several servings.

Set up two tables (or areas on the floor) where the guests will sit as two teams. Put a Bingo card and small bowl at each child's place.

Begin the Activity:

Divide the guests into two teams, not including the birthday child who will be the "caller" for the first round. Go over the rules for Bingo to be sure that all children know how to play. Decide if they have to fill their whole card to get a Bingo, or just a straight line of numbers (horizontal, vertical, diagonal).

The birthday child will begin the game as the caller for the first round. You will need to be on hand to supervise and judge any disputes, as well as keep score.

The first round begins and the game proceeds until someone calls "Bingo." The caller then verifies the numbers, and the entire table gets a round of popcorn delivered to their bowls. This encourages the table to help one another since they are winning popcorn as a team.

The child whose card was the winner becomes the next caller, and the birthday child exchanges places. Tally one point for the winning card. Continue playing until everyone has had at least one Bingo win and a turn to be the caller, or as long as the children seem involved and engaged.

At the end of the game, let the guests select a prize from the prize pack according to how many points they received.

POPPING FOR PRIZES

Category: Active
Venue: Indoor
Time: 15 minutes
Ages: 5-8
Materials:

- Large balloons (2-3 per guest)
- Wrapped prizes (1 per guest)
- Small slips of paper
- Pencil and marker
- 2 blindfolds (optional)

Preparation:
Label each wrapped prize with a numeral, using a magic marker. Put them in a large plastic trash bag.

Write a corresponding numeral on each slip of paper. Fold each small enough to insert into a balloon. Blow up and tie all the balloons and put into large trash bags to hold them safely. Some balloons will have a number slip inside, and some will not.

Begin the activity:
Have the children sit on the floor or on chairs in a circle. Tell them they are going to try to pop balloons by either stomping on them or sitting on them. If they find a number inside, they will keep it to get a prize later. Be prepared for lots of shouts and laughter.

With the birthday child going first, the children will take turns two at a time. The children whose turn it is will stand in the center of the circle while you release several of the balloons into the circle. They work to pop the balloons and see if they find a number. The children sitting in the circle will direct the balloons back into the circle if they are escaping. When the pair of poppers have popped all the released balloons, they return to the circle and another pair gets a turn. If they found a number, they will keep it with them.

Keep going in rounds, as another pair of children takes a turn and you release some more balloons. When everyone has had a turn and all the balloons are popped, everyone returns to sit in the circle. The birthday child now gets the bag of prizes and pulls one out one at a time and calls the number on the prize. The child with that number slip gets the prize and opens it.

Continue drawing prizes until the bag is empty. If a child has more than one number slip, he should give it to a child who has none. However, if he chooses, he may trade his original prize with the child who received the extra number slip.

Variations
To make the activity more challenging (and to last longer), blindfold the poppers.

RED ROVER

Category: Active

Venue: Outdoor

Time: 15-30 minutes

Ages: 8-10

Materials:

- Prizes (1 per guest)
- Kitchen timer

Preparation:

Select a large grassy area where two teams can stand across from each other with room to run. This game can get a little rough, so be sure that the guests are the kind of kids who enjoy a little roughhousing. You need to have enough guests to form two teams of four or more.

Begin the Activity:

Divide the guests into two teams. If there is a team with an odd number with more players on their team, the team with fewer players will get an extra turn. Go over any safety rules, especially that you cannot run directly into another child; you can only run into their held hands. Any violation means you go to the penalty box for one minute and your team is short one player.

The two teams stand as far apart from each other as possible, facing the other team while holding hands with arms spread out as wide as possible from each other. This leaves space for the opposing player to try to break through.

The team with the birthday child will go first. The team begins to chant:

"Red rover, red rover, send _____ right over." They insert the name of an opposing player.

The player who is chosen will run across the playing field toward the opposing team and attempt to break through the held hands and get to the other side. The opponents attempt to hold tight and prevent the runner from breaking through.

If the runner breaks through, he chooses any player to capture and return to jail behind his team. If the opposing team is successful in preventing the runner from breaking through, that player is captured and goes to their jail behind their line.

The game continues with each team taking turns calling "Red Rover" and identifying an opponent to run across. If an opponent breaks through, they can free their captured teammate and return to the team line. The game continues until one team is still holding hands with the other team captured and in jail.

The winning team gets first choice from the prize pot. The captured team can claim a consolation prize.

As time permits, rearrange the teams and play another round of the game.

RELAY RACES

Category: Active
Venue: Outdoor
Time: 15-30 minutes
Ages: 8-10
Materials:

- Rope or spray paint (washable) to mark a starting line and finish line
- 2 pillowcases
- 2 clothes baskets
- 2 each of a variety of adult size clothing items (T-shirts, shorts, socks, hats)
- Score sheet and pencil
- Prizes (1 per guest)

Preparation:
You will need a large grassy area for these relays. Mark a starting line and finish line as far away from each other as possible. Assemble the other materials.

Begin the Activity:
For each relay, divide the guests into two teams by counting off. Form new teams at the start of each relay. If there is a team with fewer children, one of the children on that team will get two turns.

Wheelbarrow Relay

The teams form two lines behind the starting line. The teams will work in pairs. One child is the wheelbarrow, and the other is the holder. They can decide which is which. The wheelbarrow child gets on her hands and the other child holds onto her partner's feet.

When both teams are ready, you will say "Ready, set, go" and the first pair from each team will proceed to the finish line and back as fast as they can, walking on hands as a wheelbarrow. When the pair gets back to the starting line, the next pair takes off. The team that gets all pairs back to the finish line first is the winner and gets a point for each player.

Pillowcase Relay

For this relay, teams work with partners to get to the finish line and back as fast as they can. Each pair puts one foot in the pillowcase and the outside foot on the ground. One hand will hold onto the pillowcase. They must cooperate by hopping or walking without falling down to get to the finish line and back. Then the next pair gets in the pillow case and takes off.

The first team to get all players back to the finish line is the winner, and earns a point for each player.

Clothesbasket Relay

You will put a basket of identical adult size large clothes (big enough to fit over the children's clothes) at the finish line, one basket opposite each team. The children line up, and when the command is given, the first child in each line runs to the clothes basket and puts on all the clothes over their own clothes. Then they run back to the start line and back to the basket where they take off all the clothes and put them back in the

basket. They then run back to their team and tap the next player to run to the clothes basket and continue the game.

The first team to get everyone back to the starting line is the winner, and each player earns a point.

Children will choose a prize from the prize pot according to the points earned.

SCAVENGER HUNT

Category: Active

Venue: Outdoor (could be Indoor as a backup)

Time: 15-30 minutes (depending on the number of items to find; the more the better).

Ages: 7-10

Materials:

- Prizes (1 for each guest)
- 2 collection bags (reusable grocery bags with handles work well)
- Kitchen timer
- 2 each of various household items such as:
  - Spoons
  - Forks
  - Pencils
  - Toothpaste tubes
  - Paper cups
  - Books
  - DVD cases
  - Measuring spoons
  - Plastic glasses
  - Small plastic storage containers
  - Etc.

Preparation:

Before the guests arrive, hide one of each item in a separate area; for example, front yard and back yard. Hide in difficult-to-find but not impossible spots. Guests will work as two teams to find the items in their playing area.

Prepare two scavenger item lists, one for each team.

Begin the activity:

Divide the guests into two teams by counting off, birthday child going first. The birthday child will be captain of his team and will choose the captain for the other team. Give each captain a collection bag and a scavenger item list. Go over the rules.

Set the timer for 15 minutes, or longer if you have many items. Say, "Ready, set, go" and the hunt begins. You will stay at home base with the timer, and also to administer the penalty box for the runners who forget the rules. You might want adult helpers out in the fields to judge any controversies.

Rules:

1. Stay within the boundaries of the game.
2. Stay with your team. Walk, don't run from place to place.
3. Those who run must return to home base and will get a one-minute penalty delay.
4. You must find the items in the order they are on the list and put them in your collection bag. If you come to an item further down the list, you should remember where it is and then come back to retrieve it when its order comes up.
5. When you have collected all the items in order, bring your collection bag back to home base for judging.

Winning the game:

The team wins by collecting all scavenger items before time runs out. Let the team that finishes first pick their prizes first.

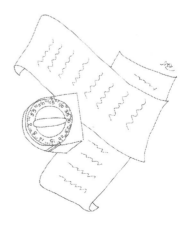

SEARCHING FOR QUESTIONS

Category: Active
Venue: Outdoor
Time: 30 minutes
Ages: 8-10
Materials:

- 1 piece of poster board
- Markers
- 1 pair of dice
- 2-5 game tokens (you can use buttons)
- 10 sheets of paper for the questions plus 1 answer sheet
- Tape or tacks to secure the question papers around the yard
- Kitchen timer
- Tally sheet and pencil for keeping score
- Prizes (1 per guest put in a bag)

Preparation:

Draw the game board on the poster board. This can be in a spiral or a grid similar to games like Chutes and Ladders or Monopoly. There should be at least 20 spaces. Write Start on the first space and Finish on the last. Put the numerals 1, 2, 3, 4, 5, 6, 7, 8, 9, 10 in various spaces, leaving some spaces for commands such as: Go back two spaces; Go ahead three spaces; Go ahead one space; Lose one turn: Wait one minute; etc.

Label the ten sheets of paper each with a numeral 1-10, large enough to be seen from a distance; about half the sheet of the paper. On the other half type or print a question. Prepare an answer sheet for yourself. Depending on the ages, make the questions appropriate to the guests' field of knowledge.

Here are some general question ideas:

1. What is the capital of our state?
2. What is the capital of our country?
3. How many eggs are in a dozen?
4. Who is the president of the United States?
5. What shape are Sponge Bob's pants?
6. How many wheels are on a bicycle?
7. Which is bigger, a softball or baseball?
8. What animal has a large trunk?
9. What do spiders weave?
10. What is the name of the planet where we live?

Make an answer key which the game director (probably you) will control.

1. Tallahassee (or your own state)
2. Washington, DC
3. Twelve
4. Barack Obama
5. Square
6. Two
7. Softball
8. Elephant
9. Web
10. Earth

Prior to the guests' arrival, attach each question sheet in locations all around the yard, the farther away from each other the better. Tack or tape them to trees, fence posts, porch railings, lawn furniture, etc. Make them difficult to find, but not impossible. You want the kids to spend time looking for them, which will also stretch out the time for the game.

Set up a table and chair somewhere in the yard as the home base area for the game director. Determine who will be the game director, either you or an adult helper. Put the game board, tokens and dice on the table.

Begin the Activity:

The children will work in teams of two (or three if there is an odd number). Number off to determine who will go together. Each team picks a game token. Determine which team goes first, second, third, etc. by rolling the die. Highest roll goes first, etc.

The first team rolls one die and moves their token that number of spaces. If they land on a numbered space, they immediately take off to find the question with that number. When they find the question and know the answer, they return to home base with their answer. They DO NOT touch the question sheet, but leave it where it is placed for the other teams to find it. The game director determines if their answer is correct. If so, they roll again and proceed with the game. If incorrect, they must try again. You can give hints if needed.

If their token lands on a space with written directions, they must do what it says. If they have to wait a certain amount of time, the game director will use a timer to determine the wait time. When time is up, they roll again.

The game director will keep a tally sheet with the teams and which questions they have answered correctly.

If a team reaches the Finish but has skipped over some questions, they must go find the questions that they skipped and report back.

Rules:
Be sure to go over the rules before the game begins.

1. Stay within the boundaries designated for the game.
2. Stay together with your team (you might make them hold hands and walk to keep things under control).
3. Do not touch or remove the question sheets. Leave them where they are.

Winning the Game:

The game ends when all teams have found and answered all ten questions. The teams get to choose a prize from the prize bag in the order in which they finish the game.

3	Go ahead 2	4	5	Lose one turn	Go Back to start
Go Back 1					6
2					Go ahead 1
1					7
Start	10	Go Back 1	9	8	Roll again

SEWING CARDS

Category: Creative
Venue: Indoor or Outdoor
Time: 15-30 minutes
Ages: 5-7
Materials:

- Thin cardboard pieces (like shirt board) about 5x7 in size (at least 1 per child)
- Crayons or markers
- Hand held hole-punch
- Yarn cut in 3-4 foot lengths with a piece of tape around one end, or shoe laces (1 per card)
- Scissors (1 per child is best)

Preparation: Cut the cardboard pieces. Place the materials in the center of the table for the children to access.

Begin the Activity:
The children sit together around a table. Each child gets a piece of cardboard and draws an object that can easily be traced. It should fill up the entire card. These could be shapes such as a triangle or circle, a Christmas tree, a snowman, a star, etc. If any child appears frustrated or confused, you can draw something for them. You can also provide a few samples for them to copy as needed.

Then the child will cut along the outline. For younger children, you may need to help with the cutting. The children will hand you their cut-outs when completed, and you will punch holes about half an inch apart along the inside border of the object. You will also tie the end of the yarn or shoe lace to secure it at the starting place.

The children will then "sew" their pictures by going in and out of the holes with their yarn or shoe lace, following the outline. If you are using yarn, wrap some cellophane tape on the sewing end so that it can easily go through the holes.

As time permits, have each child share their completed card and see if the others can guess what it is. If you are outside, some children enjoy running with the remaining string attached as if flying kites.

Write their names on the back of the cards and add them to their take-home bag.

SIMON SAYS

Category: Active (Time Filler)
Venue: Outdoor
Time: 15 minutes
Ages: 7-10
Materials:

- Rope or string for a starting line
- Score sheet and pencil
- Prizes (1 per guest)

Preparation:
Determine the playing field, which should be a large grassy area or driveway. Lay down the rope or string for the starting line.

Begin the Activity:
This classic children's game is always popular, and a good time filler as there is little preparation required. We have adapted the game so that all children stay involved rather than being eliminated as in the classic game.

The children will form a line shoulder to shoulder behind the starting line. You will be the first Simon to demonstrate a practice round. The birthday child will be the next Simon after the practice round.

Simon goes to the opposite end of the playing field and stands facing the line of children. Simon begins shouting out commands such as, "Simon says walk two giant steps; Simon says take two jumps forward; Simon says take two baby steps backwards," etc. The children all follow the commands. However, if Simon does not say "Simon says ..." and instead just gives a command such as, "Take two baby steps forward," the children should not follow the command and should stay put. Anyone who moves without first hearing "Simon says" must return to the starting line. Demonstrate how to speed up the commands to catch children moving without hearing "Simon says."

The object is for Simon to speak quickly and try to trick some children into moving when they're not supposed to and sending them back to start. The first child to reach Simon and touch him earns a point. In case of ties, each gets a point.

Continue the game with everyone getting a turn to be Simon. They can take turns by alphabetical order of first names.

At the end, everyone chooses a prize from the prize pot according to points earned. Anyone with no points gets to choose a consolation prize.

SNATCH AND GRAB

Category: Active
Venue: Outdoor
Time: 15 minutes
Ages: 5-7
Materials:

- At least 20 household objects that can be safely handled by young children (kitchen spoon, hairbrush, toothbrush, plastic drinking glass, etc.)
- 3-4 grab bags (large paper grocery bags); one per team
- Magic markers
- CD player with CD of children's songs or marching music
- Prizes (1 per guest)

Preparation:

Determine the playing field, which should be a large grassy area. Place the various objects all around the playing area in plain sight, leaving room in the middle for the children to form a circle. Make a list of all the objects so you will remember which to call out for each round. Cue up the marching music.

Begin the Activity:

The object of the game is to snatch the most objects for your team's grab bag. The children play with a partner. Have them number off by two's. If there is an odd number, one team can have three children. Give each team a grab bag and have them write their names on the outside with magic markers.

The children hold hands with their partner and form a circle facing clockwise. One partner will be on the inside and the other on the outside. Put their grab bags in the center of the circle. Before each round, you will tell the children which object they must snatch when the music stops. All the items should be in plain sight, but scattered all about, far away from each other. As the game progresses, the children will start to remember where things are for a faster snatch.

For each round, use your list to tell the children which object to snatch. They must always hold hands while hunting for the object. The first team to snatch the object comes back and puts it in their grab bag. Everyone returns to the circle for round two, and so on.

When the music starts for each round, the children march around the circle holding hands. When the music stops, they take off to find the object you have mentioned. In case of disputes of who found it first, take the object out of the game, and no one gets it.

After all the items have been snatched, the children will count how many objects are in their bag. Award prizes, with the team having the most items choosing first from the prize pot, and so on.

SNOWBALL BATTLE

(INSPIRED BY SADIE AND TATUM)

Category: Active

Venue: Outdoor or Indoor

Time: 15-30 minutes

Ages: 5-8

Materials:

- Paper towels (10-20 sheets per guest)
- Cellophane tape (1 roll per guest)
- Snowball bags (paper bags with handles, 1 per guest)
- Target (12 inch hole cut in the side of a large cardboard box)
- Chair to set the target on
- Score sheet and pencil
- Prizes (1 per guest)

Preparation:

Determine the boundaries for the snowball battle. If indoors, clear anything breakable or items like lamps that could get knocked over. This game can get a little wild.

Tear the paper towels into sheets and put in sets of 10-20 (depending on the ages, more for the older kids) around a large table or in the middle of the floor where the children will sit in a circle. Put a tape roll on top of each set. Have the snowball bags available. Set up the target in the yard or the indoor room for the game.

Begin the Activity:

Young children love to use tape. A snowball fight in summer is always a winner. Tell the children they are going to make snowballs to prepare for a snowball battle. But there will be a challenge before the battle begins.

The children sit around a table or in a circle on the floor with the snowball supplies in front. Give each child a snowball collection bag. Show the children how to wad each sheet of paper towel into a tight ball, and then cover it with tape to make it strong. At the end, they each should have 10-20 snowballs in their bag, with each child having the same number.

When everyone has their bag full, proceed to the challenge area where you have the target set up on a chair. The guests line up behind the birthday child and take a turn to throw a snowball through the target. Go to the end of the line and the next in line gets a turn. Score a point for each success. Keep throwing until everyone has used all their snowballs. Collect snowballs back in their bags.

After everyone has collected target points, the battle can begin. Let the children have free play to throw snowballs at each other. They will enjoy running around and trying to hit each other. Let the game continue as long as everyone is having fun and before it gets too rough.

At your signal, everyone stops and collects their snowballs back in their bag to take home. Then they take turns choosing a prize from the prize pot, with the guest with the most points going first.

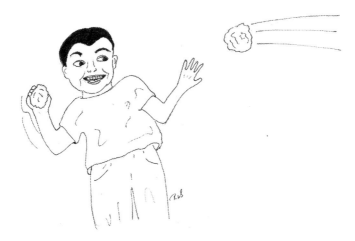

SNOWFLAKE PLACEMATS

Category: Creative
Venue: Indoor
Time: 15 minutes
Ages: 7-10
Materials:

- White printer paper cut in 6" squares (5-10 per guest)
- Scissors (1 per guest)
- Large (11"x14") construction paper in various colors (1 sheet per guest)
- Glue sticks (2 or 3 to share)

Preparation:

Cut the paper into 6" squares and put with all the materials in the center of a large table where all the children can sit. If desired, find some quiet music to play in the background as the children work.

Begin the Activity:

Show the children how to make a snowflake by demonstrating one yourself. Fold the paper into a triangle, fold again into another triangle, and snip out shapes along any of the edges. Be sure not to cut all the way through or your snowflake falls apart. After making all your desired snips, unfold and reveal your snowflake.

Let the children start making their snowflakes using two folds. After they get the idea, they can fold a third time to make a smaller triangle, resulting in more delicate patterns.

After they have made 4-6 snowflakes, they can glue them onto a piece of construction paper to make a placemat for refreshment time. You can also glue a string of snowflakes together to make a table runner.

SPEED WRAPPING

Category: Quiet Games
Venue: Indoor or Outdoor
Time: 15 minutes
Ages: 8-10
Materials:
- A variety of household objects (2 of each: brushes, combs, kitchen spoons, lotion bottles, etc.)
- 2 laundry baskets
- 2 large pillowcases or garbage bags
- Wrapping paper
- 2 rolls of cellophane tape
- Prizes (1 per guest)

Preparation:
Select a variety of household items to wrap. The more objects you have, the longer the game will last. We suggest 15 items at least. There should be two of the same item to keep the game fair. Wrap each item and place one of each pair in a separate pillowcase or garbage bag.

Begin the Activity:
The children form two teams by counting off by two's. Each team forms a line, one child behind the other, either sitting on the floor or in chairs lined up. There should be at least 10 feet of space between the two lines. The teams will line up with the birthday child first in line on one team, and the child with the closest birthday will be first in line on the second team. The children can then line up behind in alphabetical order. In case of an extra guest, that child will serve as the judge.

Put an empty clothes basket at the head of each line, with a roll of cellophane tape in each. Put the bags of wrapped items behind the last child in each line, one bag per team.

The game begins with the child at the end of the line reaching into the bag and retrieving a wrapped object. The child then speedily unwraps the object, but not tearing the paper. Then the object and the paper are passed up the line to the first child who must rewrap the object and put it in the basket. (The object must be fully wrapped with none or little of it showing.) You or the judge will decide if it passes.

The wrapper then goes to the end of the line and everyone moves up one place so there is a new wrapper in the front. The child who goes to the back retrieves the next object to unwrap and pass up the line. Continue the game until one team has successfully placed all the re-wrapped packages in their laundry basket. That team is the winner and gets to choose a prize from the prize pot.

NOTE: if the child who is trying to rewrap is having difficulty, they can get help from the teammate behind them. This teaches cooperation and teamwork.

For the consolation prize, the other team members must each guess what is inside each re-wrapped package. You hold up each wrapped object (or the judge will do it if there was an extra guest) and one at a time a guest must tell what is inside. If correct, they can choose a prize. Keep the guessing going until everyone has a chance for a prize. Other children can give hints as needed.

SPONGE BATTLE

Category: Active (and wet)
Venue: Outdoor
Time: 15 minutes
Ages: 5-10
Materials:

- Small soft round sponges (1 per guest)
- 2 large buckets filled with water
- Hose for refilling the water buckets as needed
- 2 spools of ribbon, each of a different color, cut in lengths to fit around each child's waist
- Prizes (1 per guest)

Preparation:
Note that you will need to inform guests in the invitation that they should wear a bathing suit and bring a towel. This game can also be used in conjunction with the Water Play activities in this book.

You will need a large grassy area for this game. Determine an area which will be the jail for any captured players. You might mark it off with rope or chairs. Fill the buckets with water and place one at each end of the playing area that will mark each team's home base. Have the ribbons and sponges handy.

Begin the Activity:
Divide the guests into two teams by counting off. Each team member will tie a ribbon around their waist to identify which team they are on. If there is an odd number, a team will have an extra member.

Go over the rules, boundaries and safety tips. Remind them that any-one who goes out of bounds or pushes, shoves or in any way touches another player must go to jail for a specified amount of time. You will be the judge, based on the severity of the offense. Show them where to find the hose to add more water to their team bucket if they need it.

The object of the game is to send players on the opposing team to jail by hitting them with a wet sponge. The game ends when one team is successful in jailing all the others at least once, or when time expires.

Give each child a sponge. Players go to their buckets and load up by soaking their sponge in the bucket of water. At your command to start, the teams proceed to the playing field to start the battle. They throw their sponges at members of the opposing team, identified by the color of ribbon, while also trying to escape getting hit themselves.

If a player gets sponged by the opposing team, he or she must go to jail. They stay there and count aloud to ten or more, depending on the children's ages. You will act as the jail guard who releases them after they have completed their counted out sentence to return to the battle. Players can return at any time to their team's bucket to reload their sponge with water.

At the end of the official battle, you can let the children run around freely throwing their sponges. They may enjoy this even more than the structured play. Use your judgment.

Children will select prizes from the prize pot according to which team captured the most prisoners. You can use the honor system to have the children self-report how many times they went to jail.

THE RING ON THE STRING

Category: Quiet games
Venue: Indoor
Time: 15 minutes
Ages: 8-10
Materials:

- Prizes (1 per guest)
- 1 large piece of sturdy twine long enough to make one large circle, depending on number of guests
- 1 adult size finger ring
- Score sheet and pencil

Preparation:
Put one end of the twine through the ring and tie the ends of the string together.

Begin the Activity:
The children will stand in a circle facing in; close enough to each other to be able to pass the ring to the next person. The birthday child will go to the center of the circle.

The other children each will grasp the string with both hands, palms facing down. One child will be holding the ring on the string, hiding it from view.

The game begins with the children sliding their hands back and forth on the string, and attempting to pass the ring from person to person without being detected. The child in the middle must close his or her eyes and count to ten while turning around before trying to guess who has the ring.

The object is for the child in the center to guess where the ring is within five tries. The guesser points to a specific hand, and the hider opens the hand to reveal the ring (or not).

If the child in the center finds the ring within five guesses, he or she gets a point and changes places with the child who last had the ring. If the child in the center cannot find the ring, he or she gets no points while all the others who successfully hid the ring each get a point. The center child exchanges places with the child who has the ring.

Continue until everyone has a turn in the center, or as long as the children are having fun. Award prizes according to the number of points collected. Anyone with no points can get a consolation prize.

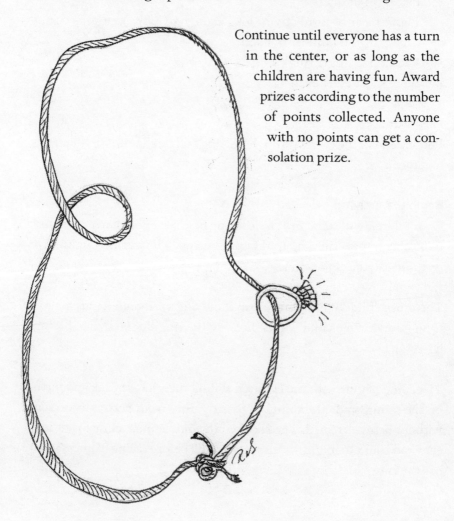

WATER PLAY

Category: Active
Venue: Outdoor
Time: 30 minutes
Ages: 5-10
Materials:

- Prizes (at least 1 per guest)
- Sprinkler and hose
- Squirt guns (1 per guest)
- Water balloons (5 per guest)
- Long vinyl sheet or Slip and Slide game
- Kitchen timer
- Score sheet and pencil

Preparation:

All children enjoy water play when the weather is hot. When you send out invitations, let the guests know that they should wear a bathing suit and bring a towel. You will also want to serve the birthday cake and open presents outside since the children will be in wet bathing suits.

Fill the water balloons and put in a large wastebasket or garbage can. Determine the playing field, which should be a large grassy area.

Begin the Activities:

It's best to divide the activities into ten-minute segments. For the first ten minutes, turn on the sprinkler and let the children run through. Next bring out the squirt guns and the children can chase each other while trying to squirt each other for ten minutes. When that gets old, start the Slip and Slide with the children lining up and taking turns sliding to the end for ten minutes.

Finally, start the water balloon contest. There will be prizes for this game. The object is to get the fewest points, with zero being the best. The children compete in pairs, tossing back and forth to one another. Remind the children that they will use underhanded tosses.

Set the timer for 10 minutes. The children count off by two's to make two lines, facing across from another child about three feet apart. Each child on one side gets a water balloon and tosses it to the child across. After each toss, they must each step back one foot. Keep tossing and stepping back until they miss. If the balloon bursts they get a new water balloon and must start over. If it drops but does not burst, they can pick it up and keep going.

After a couple of rounds, you can change the pairs to have new partners, especially if one pair seems to be having trouble throwing and catching.

Every time a pair misses the catch and the balloon bursts, they each score one point. At the end of the timeframe when the timer goes off, each pair with fewer than 5 points wins a prize. If any pair scores zero points, they are declared the champion(s) and can get a special prize or an extra prize.

BIBLIOGRAPHY

Best New Games by Dale N. LeFevre, Human Kinetics (2002)

Birthday Parties, Best Tips & Ideas by Vicki Lansky, Book Peddlers (2003)

The Cokesbury Game Book (revised) by Arthur M. Depew, Abingdon Press (1960)

Motherhood Smotherhood by JJ Keith, Skyhorse Publishing (2014)

The Opposite of Spoiled by Ron Lieber, Harper (2015)

ABOUT THE AUTHORS

The authors are a mother and daughter team...

Mother and Grandma

Dr. Sarah (Sally) Butzin, PhD, is a retired educator who has won numerous awards for her teaching and research work. Her book, *Joyful classrooms in an age of accountability: The Project CHILD recipe for success,* was published in 2005. She is the author of numerous published articles, and developer of the Project CHILD (Changing How Instruction for Learning is Delivered) instructional system which has been used in elementary schools throughout the country. Many of the ideas and activities in this book have been derived from her work as an elementary school teacher and product developer, as well as her experiences as a summer camp program director.

She retired in 2011 as the founder and Executive Director of the Institute for School Innovation in Tallahassee, Florida. She remains active with golf, writing and volunteer work, serving as Chair of the Board of Trustees of the International Alliance for Invitational Education (www. invitationaleducation.net).

Sally lives in Tallahassee and is married to Peter Butzin. In addition to Charlotte, they have another daughter, Jessica Butzin O'Reilly, who resides in Irvington, New York, with husband Paul and children Madeline and Charlotte.

Daughter and Mom

Charlotte Butzin Beal is Editorial Consultant at CEB Iconoculture, a consumer insights company that delivers to marketers important shifts in people's values, desires and behaviors (www.iconoculture.com). She previously served as an associate editor at *Bon Appétit* magazine.

Charlotte lives in Burbank, California, with her TV-editor husband Josh Beal and two children – daughter Sadie and son Tatum. Charlotte is an accomplished chef who enjoys creating interesting and nutritious meals for her family. She is also a film buff.

Attending multiple modern-day kids' birthday parties, along with her knowledge about what consumers really want and are ready for, inspired her to write this book with her mom.

ABOUT THE ILLUSTRATOR

Robert (Bob) W. Smith grew up in Miami and has been creative since childhood. He and his three brothers, two sisters and parents shared many artistic talents. Bob has drawn and/or painted images from memory as well as photographs, and loves to take the client's ideas and bring them to life. This is the second book he has illustrated and he has a third book on the drawing table. His motto is, "You are only limited by your imagination."

Bob lives in Tallahassee with his wife, Debbie. He worked in the banking industry for almost 30 years, earned a Masters of Social Work degree and now works full time in a local cancer center. He also enjoys playing several musical instruments, gardening, reading and cooking. He and Debbie have two grown children in Tallahassee and two small dogs.

Printed in the United States
By Bookmasters